MOON METRO

CONTENTS

INTRODUCTION

A DAY IN WASHINGTON D.C.

NEIGHBORHOOD MAPS

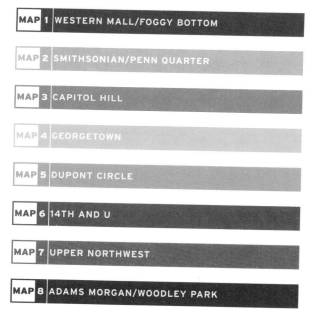

WASHINGTON D.C.

HOW TO USE THIS BOOK

MAP SECTION

- We've divided Washington D.C. into eight distinct areas. Each area has been assigned a color, used on the map itself and in easy-to-spot map number indicators throughout the listings.

- The maps show the location of every listing in the book, using the icon that indicates what type of listing it is (sight, restaurant, etc.) and the listing's locator number.

- The coordinates (in color) indicate the specific grid that the listing is located in. The black number is the listing's locator number. The page number directs you to the listing's full description.

LISTINGS SECTION

- Listings are organized into six sections:

  - ❂ SIGHTS
  - ℞ RESTAURANTS
  - ◓ NIGHTLIFE
  - ❂ SHOPS
  - ❹ ARTS AND LEISURE
  - ℍ HOTELS

- Within each section, listings are organized by which map they are located in, then in alphabetical order.

- Look for ◖ to find recommended sights, restaurants, nightlife, shops, arts and leisure, and hotels.

MAP 5 DUPONT CIRCLE

AL TIRAMISU ROMANTIC • ITALIAN $$$
This Dupont Circle hideaway serves up scrumptious Italian favorites – black truffles, imported branzino, and duck with balsamic vinegar and honey sauce, for example – in cozy booths that are perfect for a romantic tryst. Beware: the luscious specials are sure to induce sticker shock.

MAP 5 B4 ◖25 2014 P ST. NW
202-467-4466   WWW.ALTIRAMISU.COM

BLUE DUCK TAVERN BUSINESS • AMERICAN $$$
At this Tony Chi-designed neighborhood grill, the kitchen isn't all that's out in the open. Farm-fresh produce and freshly caught seafood appears on the menu complete with region of origin and where it was harvested.

MAP 5 D3 ◖45 1201 24TH ST. NW
202-419-6755   WWW.BLUEDUCKTAVERN.COM

DISH HOT SPOTS • AMERICAN $$$
Dish, at the homey River Inn, is a whimsical tribute to American cooking. Everything here, from the classic meatloaf to the brassy BLT, tastes like something Mom used to make, only better. In the winter, enjoy dinner by the roaring fireplace.

MAP 5 E3 ◖60 THE RIVER INN, 924 25TH ST. NW
202-338-8707   WWW.THERIVERINN.COM

FAMOUS LUIGI'S ROMANTIC • ITALIAN $$
Red-checkered tablecloths, free-flowing wine, and a strolling flower salesman – Luigi's is straight out of The Godfather. Dine on hearty portions of garlicky red-sauce fare inside the dark, noisy dining room or on the roomier glass-encased porch. On busy weekend nights, takeout pizza and pasta is the way to go.

MAP 5 D5 ◖50 132 19TH ST. NW
202-331-7574   WWW.FAMOUSLUIGIS.COM

GALILEO BUSINESS • ITALIAN $$$
Always one of Washington's hottest reservations (and more popular than ever since Roberto Donna's appearances on Iron Chef America), Galileo draws politicos, power couples, and expense-account types with fine northern Italian cuisine and a formal dining atmosphere. The dinner-only osteria offers the same quality cuisine for bargain prices.

MAP 5 D4 ◖48 1110 21ST ST. NW
202-293-7191   WWW.GALILEODC.COM

KAZ SUSHI BISTRO BUSINESS • SUSHI $$$
Renowned sushi chef Kaz Okochi tackles traditional sushi with a creative hand, often pairing the best of East and West. Beyond sushi, the menu presents several grilled specialties and artful bento boxes of tempura, rice, and meat. The cool, jade Asian decor sets a lovely scene.

MAP 5 E3 ◖62 1915 I ST. NW
202-530-5500   WWW.KAZSUSHIBISTRO.COM

30 MOON METRO

← TWO WAYS TO NAVIGATE →

1. Scan the map to see what listings are in the area you want to explore. Use the directory to find out the name and page number for each listing.

2. Read the listings to find the specific place you want to visit. Use the map information at the bottom of each listing to find the listing's exact location.

MAP KEY

Major Sights	★
Metro Stop	Ⓜ
Shopping District	———
Stairs	ⅢⅢⅢⅢⅢ
Pedestrian Street	———
Adjacent Map Boundaries	SEE MAP 1

SECTION ICONS

⊙ SIGHTS

Ⓡ RESTAURANTS

Ⓝ NIGHTLIFE

⊙ SHOPS

Ⓐ ARTS AND LEISURE

Ⓗ HOTELS

RESTAURANTS

GALILEO   KRAMERBOOKS & AFTERWORDS

KRAMERBOOKS & AFTERWORDS *AFTER HOURS • AMERICAN* $$
This bookstore/café is better for browsing than grazing, but it's still a big draw for the black-turtleneck crowd. Discuss Kafka and capitalism with your fellow literati, then browse the store and stay to write while ...

LUNA GRILL ...
It's eggs and ...
fee shop. Vege...
make-your-own...
of comfort food...
the spot.

MARCEL'S ...
Chef/owner R...
working culina...
ful yet casual ...
with the likes ...
crisped-sp...

202-296-1166 WWW.MARCELSDC.COM

MARK AND ORLANDO'S *HOT SPOTS • AMERICAN* $$$
Downstairs, Mark serves cheeseburgers and crab cakes. Upstairs, Orlando handles upscale offerings such as mahimahi and venison. Thanks to the varied menu and chipper service, this split-level row house with a split personality is a hit among its diverse Dupont clientele of young and old, hipster and CEO.
B4 ❸ **23** 2020 P ST. NW 202-223-8463 WWW.MARKANDORLANDOS.COM

OBELISK *ROMANTIC • ITALIAN* $$$
This is one of the city's finest purveyors of Italian countryside cooking. Delicious seasonal ingredients and a dedicated staff give the simple dining room a familiar vibe. The five-course, prix-fixe menu lures repeat customers both young and old.
B4 ❸ **21** 2029 P ST. NW 202-872-1180

BLUE DUCK TAVERN *BUSINESS • AMERICAN* $$$
At this Tony Chi-designed neighborhood grill, the kitchen isn't all that's out in the open. Farm-fresh produce and freshly caught seafood appears on the menu complete with region of origin and where it was harvested.

MAP 5 D3 Ⓡ 45   1201 24TH ST. NW
202-419-6755   WWW.BLUEDUCKTAVERN.COM

Use the **MAP NUMBER, COLOR GRID COORDINATES,** and **BLACK LOCATOR NUMBER** to find the exact location of every listing in the book.

31

INTRODUCTION TO
WASHINGTON D.C.

Washington D.C. is a city of low-rise buildings and sky-scraper-sized egos. It is a place where campaign managers get rock star treatment, every barroom TV in town is tuned to CNN (or Fox News), and even your cab driver is anxious to talk politics. It's a city without a state, with taxation (but without representation), where all roads literally lead to Capitol Hill, the city center. In many ways, the place is a riddle. And if you're here in August, the joke will be on you: Washington was built on a swamp, so central air-conditioning will seem more important than a voter registration card.

The city is also the gateway to the South, with acres of public parkland and historic estates. John F. Kennedy once complained about the city's "Southern efficiency," but that was a while ago. The corporate culture here demands that things run like military clockwork. The Metro is spotless and punctual, and some heavily traveled streets become one-way every rush hour – to the relief of local commuters and to the confusion of frazzled out-of-towners. Security has been ramped up since September 11, 2001, and it's not unusual to see checkpoints in front of important buildings.

Despite the trauma of 9/11, Washington has settled back into a routine. Government workers often clock out by 6 P.M., and downtown streets tend to clear out. Power players duck into expense-account dining rooms, people young and old crowd the Mall to play volleyball or baseball, and others begin the trek

D.C.'S HEART AND SOUL

Politics might drive Washington's mind, but its heart and soul belong to the African American tradition. About 60 percent of the city's residents are black, and their heritage predates the District's founding in 1791. As a Southern city, Washington once held slave markets on what is now the National Mall. Decades later, Georgetown was a prominent stop on the Underground Railroad. In the 20th century, civil rights rallies electrified the city.

Today, this heritage is preserved in many sights, such as the African American Civil War Memorial that lists every black American who fought in that war, the newly christened Marvin Gaye Park, and the Lincoln Memorial, where Martin Luther King Jr.'s "I Have a Dream" speech is etched on the steps. The rich tradition also steers the city's cultural life. Washington swells with world-class jazz and blues clubs, shops selling traditional African clothing and furniture, and museums dedicated to African American history, music, and even fashion. The country's best Ethiopian and Eritrean food is served in Adams Morgan – just steps from the Duke Ellington Bridge, named after one of D.C.'s most famous sons.

back uptown. Many residents step out of the Metro at Dupont Circle, Adams Morgan, or U Street, areas full of bars, shops, and ethnic restaurants of every persuasion. In these vibrant neighborhoods, with dignified townhouses on every corner and sidewalks teeming with businesspeople, briefcase in hand and cell phone glued to ear, it might seem that there is no limit to the wealth and power concentrated here.

On the other side of the Capitol, however, the neighborhoods of Northeast and Southeast Washington struggle in its shadow. Many people never venture to this side of the city, alarmed by constant reports of violent crime. Those who do will find some of Washington's most beautiful row houses, best Southern restaurants, and lushest gardens next to crumbling buildings and vacant lots. Residents are fiercely loyal to their neighborhoods and to their politicians – despite a scandal-plagued run as mayor, Marion Barry won a city council seat in 2004 with an overwhelming majority. Many families have been here for generations, regardless of who's in office.

But the bulk of the major sights are back in North- and Southwest, where D.C. seems like an orderly city of energetic transients. Year after year, bright-eyed idealists arrive ready to change the world. Many do, and many end up moving on after leaving their mark. So the faces pouring through the streets change every few years, each wanting to influence legislation, pass this bill, seal that deal. Meanwhile, the Washington Monument, the White House, the Capitol – icons that have welcomed generations of young hopefuls – stand tall in all their grandeur, patiently waiting for the next world leader to arrive.

HISTORY

Washington D.C. began as – what else? – a political disagreement. After the Revolutionary War, Northerners favored New York City or Philadelphia as the center of power. But Southern politicians wanted a capital closer to them and offered up land and money to get their way. If the Northern states agreed to establish the capital farther south, it was decided, the federal government would assume the war debts of all the states. In the end, Congress approved the Compromise of 1790, and Charles Pierre L'Enfant designed Washington D.C. in a then-innovative grid system. John Adams was the first president to live in the Executive Mansion, which was constantly under construction during his presidency – as was much of the city.

For years afterward, Washington was a quiet town with a tiny population, but it began to look and feel like a modern city after the Civil War. The population swelled, monuments were built, and the stage was set for the city to become the backdrop for the tumultuous 20th century. The National Mall was a prime protest scene during the Civil Rights struggle and the Vietnam War, and Martin Luther King Jr.'s "I Have a Dream" speech became immortal at the Lincoln Memorial in 1963. Watergate was a historic moment of a different kind, and the chic hotel-office complex that helped ruin Richard Nixon in 1974 still stands. Today, D.C. is a booming metropolis surrounded by endless suburban sprawl, still rich with political squabbles and plenty of scandal.

DON'T SNACK AND RIDE

Most everyone gets around on the Metro, D.C.'s subway system, which is clean and famously efficient. (Hardened commuters joke that they can hear the Metro's jarring "Doors closing!" recording even in their sleep.) By and large, Metro stations are safe – except for snackers. Eating, drinking, smoking, and littering are prohibited, and Metro officials are always on the alert for violations. Police have detained travelers caught eating inside stations or onboard the train. One rider was arrested for unwrapping a candy bar while on an escalator and refusing to discard it. The results of this vigilance are visible: The platforms and surrounding areas are spotless.

THE WHITE HOUSE   OLD EBBITT GRILL   LINCOLN MEMORIAL

THE BEST OF
WASHINGTON D.C.

With all that D.C. has to offer, a day in the capital can mean breakfasting among White House staffers, viewing the newest memorial on the Mall, touching a moon rock, and enjoying dinner at a talk-of-the-town restaurant. Breathtaking sights like the Washington Monument and the Lincoln Memorial have long been necessary stops for any visitor. And an afternoon at one of the Smithsonian museums is worth about a year in college – and costs a lot less. Here is a day that samples classic D.C., full of those must-see landmarks that still take even native Washingtonians by pleasant surprise.

1 Have a quintessential Washington breakfast downtown at the **Old Ebbitt Grill (p. 23),** where the power players often meet.

2 Work off your meal with a stroll down Pennsylvania Avenue to the **White House (p. 7)** for some choice photo opportunities from the Ellipse.

3 From the White House, the National Mall is a quick and scenic walk away. If you've reserved tickets (or were willing to wait in line from an absurdly early hour), take a ride to the top of the **Washington Monument (p. 6)** for a panoramic view of the city.

4 Explore the western part of the Mall's many monuments and memorials – the new-in-2004 **National World War II Memorial (p. 3)** is a must. Afterward, grab a quick lunch from one of the many vendors scattered around the perimeter – they sell everything from pizza and hot dogs to egg rolls.

[5] At the opposite end of the Mall is the **Smithsonian Institution (p. 12).** Spend the afternoon exploring one or two of its several museums: The **National Air and Space Museum (p. 9)** is always a favorite.

[6] Stroll away from the Mall into bustling Penn Quarter to visit the **Reynolds Center (p. 68),** the Smithsonian's American art museum that reopened in 2006 after years of renovation.

[7] The nearby **IndeBleu (p. 25),** offering more than 50 specialty cocktails, is a good stop for early evening drinks.

[8] For dinner, head into Chinatown for glamorous Asian-Latin fusion at **Zengo D.C. (p. 26).**

[9] Take a cab back toward the National Mall area for a look at the monuments after dark. The **Lincoln Memorial (p. 2)** is luminescent at night, not to mention less crowded.

[10] After a full day of sightseeing, hop back into the cab and head to U Street to unwind the way many locals do: listening to live music. Pop into **Cafe Nema (p. 46)** for jazz and hip-hop (and no cover charge), or squeeze into **Café Saint Ex/Gate 54 (p. 46)** to hear the city's best DJs spin.

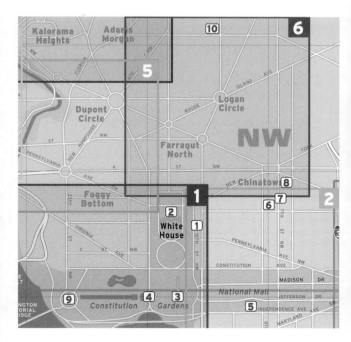

NATIONAL ZOO   KRAMERBOOKS & AFTERWORDS

OFF-THE-MALL
WASHINGTON D.C.

From the lobbyists on K Street to the politicians on the Hill, Washington is, to a large degree, a high-powered destination. But this buttoned-up city is loosening its tie more and more. Sleek boutique hotels and edgy restaurants continue to pop up around town, making it possible to fill up a day in the city without visiting a single monument. Of course, there can be no substitution for some Washington institutions, such as the venerable jazz venue HR-57 and the late-night, heartburn-inducing Ben's Chili Bowl.

1 Start at **Hotel Palomar (p. 92),** the posh hideaway off Dupont Circle where you've booked your stay.

2 Stroll toward Dupont, and grab brunch on the patio of **Kramerbooks & Afterwords (p. 31),** a favorite hipster hangout. After eating, browse through the bookstore – the travel and cookbook sections are particularly notable.

3 Spend the morning shopping the chic boutiques and upmarket chains of **Dupont Circle (p. 59).** You'll also find a bead shop (Beadazzled) and an indie record store (Melody Records) in this area.

4 Continue your retail therapy with a walk up **18th Street (p. 63)** to check out Adams Morgan's many eclectic shops, where the items on offer range from the latest fashions to antique doorknobs.

5 Washington has some of the best Ethiopian restaurants in the country, and many of them can be found in Adams Morgan. Savor an authentic lunch at **Meskerem (p. 39)** on 18th Street.

6 The **National Zoo (p. 19)** is an easy walk or short cab ride from the restaurant. You may be magnetically drawn to the Giant Panda Habitat, as most visitors are, but don't miss the other thousands of animals here.

7 Catch the Metro at Woodley Park and take it to U Street/Cardozo. Peek in the windows of the funky boutiques along U Street on the way to **Crème Café (p. 34)** for some homey soul food.

8 After dinner, duck into **Tabaq Bistro (p. 47),** one of D.C.'s most buzzed-about bars. Sip libations by candlelight in the subterranean lounge, or venture upstairs for spectacular views of the city from the glass-encased terrace.

9 Head around the corner to **HR-57 (p. 79).** Named after a House resolution to make jazz a national treasure, this institution showcases amazing live music.

10 Before heading to bed, satisfy late-night hunger pangs with a hot dog or chili from **Ben's Chili Bowl (p. 34),** an eye-opener at any hour of the day.

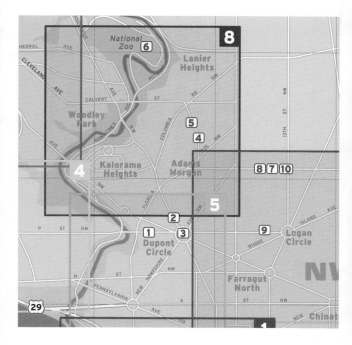

FORD'S THEATRE INTERNATIONAL SPY MUSEUM

WASHINGTON D.C.
CONFIDENTIAL

Scandal and intrigue have enshrouded Washington since its early days as the capital city, when shocked locals whispered about Abigail Adams hanging her laundry in the unfinished East Room of the White House. Over the years, the topics of rumor and investigation have ranged from the everyday affairs of Senators to international espionage. The following offers a glimpse into Washington's underworld.

1 Begin your day in **Georgetown (p. 57),** home to many of Washington's politicians and spies. Alger Hiss, the focus of a notorious espionage case in the late 1940s, is among the significant figures that have lived here. Spend the morning shopping along M Street.

2 Enjoy a civilized Italian lunch at **Café Milano (p. 28),** a beloved haunt for Washington's "cave dwellers" – a nickname for those who have been established in the city for generations. This is a favorite of local socialites, so try to listen for some hot gossip.

3 Spend a few hours in popular **Rock Creek National Park (p. 87),** easily accessed via the Woodley Park or Cleveland Park Metro stops. This serene green expanse may hold some dark secrets: Klingle Mansion, located in a remote area of the park, was a hub of investigations into intern Chandra Levy's mysterious disappearance in 2001.

4 For an indoor adventure, take the Metro again, this time to Gallery Place-Chinatown, and head to D.C.'s homage to scandal and intrigue: the **International Spy Museum (p. 68).** History, gadgets, and video of former spies are displayed in the fascinating exhibits here.

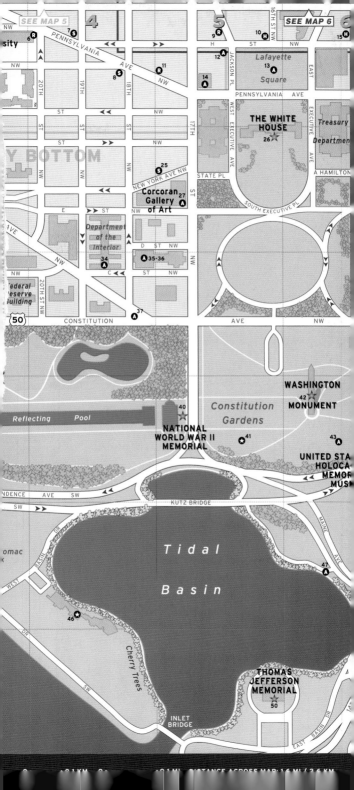

5 Make a detour to the **United States Capitol (p. 14),** an easy walk or a quick Metro ride away. This hallowed complex, which includes the House and Senate office buildings, has seen scandals from both sides: Committees have investigated them, and representatives have been implicated in them. The building, with its gorgeous dome, is always ready for a photo-op.

6 Make plans for a hearty dinner at the nearby **Charlie Palmer Steak (p. 27).** Its proximity to the Capitol makes it a reliable location for big-wig and deal-maker sightings – see who you can spot.

7 After steaks, return to Penn Quarter and settle in for a show at **Ford's Theatre (p. 77),** where Abraham Lincoln was shot. John Wilkes Booth is known as the assassin by school children across the land, but was there a larger conspiracy at work?

8 Before turning in, stop at **Prime Rib (p. 32)** for a nightcap. Popular among power players, this steakhouse was a favorite pick-up destination for Jessica Cutler, the Capitol Hill staffer who gained notoriety in 2004 for chronicling her steamy liaisons with top pols online.

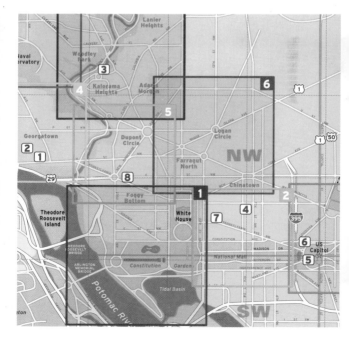

MAP 1 WESTERN MALL/FOGGY BOTTOM

WESTERN MALL/ FOGGY BOTTOM

The western part of the Mall is a rite of passage for tourists, school groups, and history buffs. The Washington Monument marks the eastern edge of this memorial-heavy area, where tributes to Abraham Lincoln and the veterans of World War II, Korea, and Vietnam each take their place around the more than 2,000-foot-long Reflecting Pool. Farther south, by the Tidal Basin, are the Franklin Delano Roosevelt Memorial and the Thomas Jefferson Memorial. Springtime is *sakura* season, and the expanse brightens with lush pink cherry blossoms. This is Washington at its best and most beautiful, combining aesthetic appeal with a strong sense of history.

To the north, Foggy Bottom is the rare neighborhood where college students and upscale Washingtonians peacefully coexist. The John F. Kennedy Center for the Performing Arts and posh Watergate Complex hug the edge of the Potomac, and these blocks are also George Washington University's unofficial campus. Classroom buildings are interspersed with well-kept townhouses. However, the sleepy neighborhood isn't always serene: The White House, World Bank, and International Monetary Fund are also nearby, so protestors know the area well.

MAP 1 WESTERN MALL/FOGGY BOTTOM

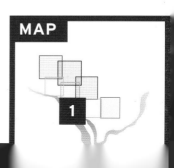

MAP

1

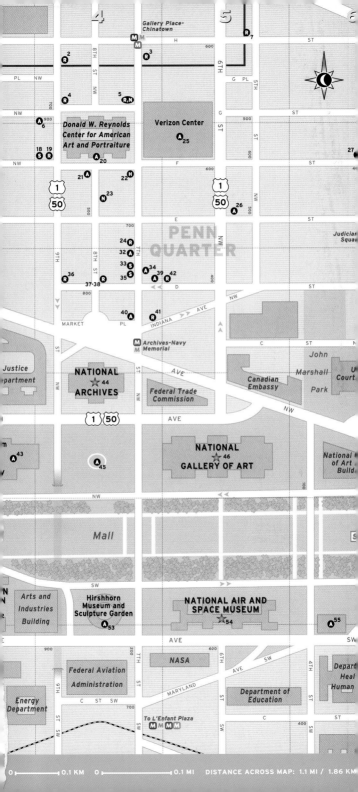

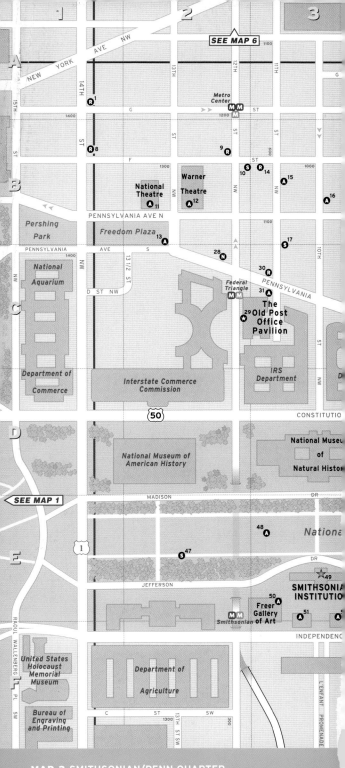

NEW YORK AVE NW

14TH ST

13TH ST

12TH ST

11TH ST

15TH ST

G

Metro
Center
Ⓜ Ⓜ ST

1400

F

G

1200

1000

600

Ⓡ 1

A

Ⓡ 8

1300

9 Ⓡ

Ⓢ
10

Ⓡ 14

Ⓐ 15

Ⓐ 16

B

National
Theatre
Ⓐ 11

Warner
Theatre
Ⓐ 12

NW

NW

NW

PENNSYLVANIA AVE N

Pershing
Park

Freedom Plaza
13
Ⓐ

1100

Ⓢ 17

PENNSYLVANIA

AVE

S

28
Ⓝ

10TH ST

National
Aquarium

13 1/2 ST

D ST NW

30
PENNSYLVANIA

Federal
Triangle
Ⓜ Ⓜ

31 ★

29 ★

The
Old Post
Office
Pavilion

C

1400

NW

NW

Department
of
Commerce

Interstate Commerce
Commission

IRS
Department

ST

NW

D

🛣 50

CONSTITUTIO

D

National Museum of
American History

National Museu
of
Natural Histo

◀ SEE MAP 1

MADISON

DR

1

48
Ⓐ

Nationa

E

🛣 1

Ⓢ 47

DR

49 ★

JEFFERSON

SMITHSONIA
INSTITUTIO

RAOUL WALLENBERG PL SW

50
Freer
Gallery
of Art

Ⓜ Ⓜ
Smithsonian

Ⓐ 51

Ⓐ

INDEPENDENC

United States
Holocaust
Memorial
Museum

Department
of
Agriculture

L'ENFANT PROMENADE

Bureau of
Engraving
and Printing

C

ST

SW

1300

13TH ST SW

300

MAP 2 SMITHSONIAN/PENN QUARTER

SMITHSONIAN/ PENN QUARTER

The stately buildings of the Smithsonian border the National Mall between 3rd and 14th Streets. These blocks are lined with museums, among them the exceptionally popular National Air and Space Museum. Venturing north into downtown, the National Archives showcase the Constitution and the Declaration of Independence in high-tech – and high-security – displays.

After a day of museum-hopping, Penn Quarter is the ideal place to unwind. These once-desolate streets now boast some of the finest supping and sipping in the city, with lines forming out the door for hot spots like IndeBleu, Jaleo, and Zaytinya. Some of Washington's most notable theaters are nearby, as are the Verizon Center and the International Spy Museum.

North of the Verizon Center, Chinatown is Washington's amazing shrinking neighborhood. The once-humble ethnic enclave now looks increasingly like a mini-Times Square as shopping-mall chains commandeer every block. Nonetheless, Chinatown's ornate arch still stands, and modest restaurants like Full Kee lure lunchtime crowds, unfazed by the intrusion of the likes of Hooters and Ruby Tuesday.

MAP 2 SMITHSONIAN/PENN QUARTER

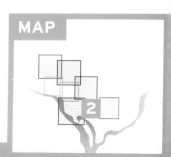

MAP

2

CAPITOL HILL

During working hours, Capitol Hill is a staid model of dignity. This is where you'll find congressional office buildings, the marble steps of the Supreme Court, and the imposing Library of Congress. This is also the literal center of Washington D.C.: the Northwest, Northeast, Southwest, and Southeast sections of the city radiate out from the rotunda-crowned Capitol building. But many government toilers (and famous politicos) make their homes here as well. By and large, the Hill is a quaint blend of comfort and style: Sleek restaurants and bars merrily share turf with funky cafés and refurbished brownstones.

Just blocks from the Hill to the southeast is the Eastern Market. Swarming with street vendors nearly every weekend, it draws young families and couples stocking up on fresh food, flowers, and knick-knacks for their chic brownstones. Saturday and Sunday mornings are the best time to get a taste of this very local experience.

North of the Capitol, Union Station greets a steady stream of local commuters and out-of-town travelers. When it opened in 1907, it was the world's largest train station. Today, it still functions as a travel gateway, but it's also a destination in itself: The Beaux-Arts building is filled with shops, restaurants, and a nine-screen movie theater.

MAP 3 CAPITOL HILL

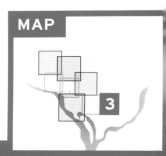

MAP

3

GEORGETOWN

Despite the emergence of hipster chains like Intermix, Mexx, and H&M, Georgetown is still a bona fide preppy mecca, with cute cafés, designer boutiques, and art galleries that charm the social-register set. The mansions are plentiful, the streets are mostly cobblestone, and the hair on the ladies who lunch is as stiff as your waiter's collared shirt. M Street is the center of all the retail action, but there's also history in the midst of all the storefronts. Washington's oldest building, the 1765 Old Stone House, sits among shops such as Victoria's Secret and Barnes & Noble. The neighborhood is also home to Georgetown University; students are easy to identify by their good looks – and sometimes by their illegally parked BMWs.

Also sharing this area is Dumbarton Oaks, the site of the famous 1944 conferences that ultimately led to the creation of the United Nations. Outside, the 10 acres of gardens are breathtaking in any season.

With all these attractions and no Metro stop, Georgetown has its share of traffic and parking headaches. Take a cab, try the 30-minute walk from the Dupont Circle or Foggy Bottom Metro station, or hop on the Georgetown Metro Connection, a shuttle bus ($1 one-way) that travels to and from either Metro station every 10 minutes.

MAP 4 GEORGETOWN

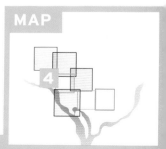

MAP

4

DUPONT CIRCLE

Dupont Circle is more than simply a crowded rotary. At the center of the circle is a grassy park frequented by poets, protestors, and college students, and the neighborhood surrounding it is Washington's cultural heart.

Gay life has thrived here since the post-Stonewall 1970s, and many surrounding shops proudly display pride flags, welcoming customers from all walks of life. The upscale restaurants and townhouses cater to scenesters, whereas secondhand clothing stores, family-owned bookstores, and record shops make the indie crowd feel right at home, too. Dupont is Washington at its most carefree and eclectic.

South of the circle, but north of Foggy Bottom, lies K Street, an imposing thoroughfare where most of D.C.'s political scandals, smear campaigns, and spin cycles come into being. Lobbying firms, law firms, political consulting firms... if it's corporate, chances are it's on K Street. The sensation of power is electrifying: Saunter down the street, and just try not to get mowed over by the frantic march of professionals, power-walking to their next meeting. Accordingly, some of the city's most decadent expense-account restaurants are in this neighborhood. Pull up a seat at Prime Rib, the city's quintessential steakhouse, and spy the power players who strut through the door.

MAP 5 DUPONT CIRCLE

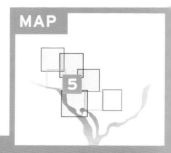

MAP

5

14TH AND U

These two streets and the surrounding area continue to evolve from forgotten ghetto to D.C.'s hottest up-and-coming neighborhood. Former houses of ill repute have been restored to their Victorian splendor, and sleek luxury condos lure wealthy worker bees.

Constantly expanding with shops and restaurants, 14th Street has breathed fresh life into the local economy. New pubs and eateries are springing up throughout the neighborhood, and the Whole Foods market on P Street has made the gentrification official.

To the north, U Street is an urban success story. The street was once a grand strip of African American music clubs, theaters, and stately residences. But encroaching poverty and violence drove many families away, and for years the street was deserted and run-down. But for years now, it's been Washington's most toothsome address. The growth of gourmet restaurants, bakeries, vintage clothing shops, and swanky lounges has made U Street a hip destination with history and soul. Despite the influx of new business, however, some things on U Street haven't changed. No one ever dared mess with Ben's Chili Bowl, the beloved diner that has cured generations of Washington's hangovers.

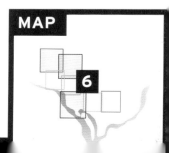

MAP 6

UPPER NORTHWEST

Once considered an outlying district perfect for a summer home, the Upper Northwest of today is just a few short Metro stops from the center of D.C. The area is semi-suburban, with housing ranging from multimillion-dollar estates with sprawling lawns to apartments and condos for the younger set.

The most interesting area for visitors is Cleveland Park, situated along Connecticut Avenue. This comfortable residential strip is notable for its excellent restaurants as well as the city's finest movie theater, the Uptown. Weekends, you'll find older families and twentysomethings dining side-by-side at Spices or Palena, two of the city's best restaurants, or sipping cocktails at Bardeo's new rooftop bar.

The English Gothic–style Washington National Cathedral is another reason to make the trek from the Mall. Perched on a hill 676 feet above sea level, it makes for great city views. South of the cathedral, on Massachusetts Avenue, is the Naval Observatory, where the vice president resides. This area is a popular venue for protestors of all stripes (and hostility levels). A little farther down the avenue, more than 50 foreign embassies line Embassy Row. A walk or drive down this grand boulevard offers up an eclectic mix of mansions and a chance to count how many countries' flags you can identify by sight.

MAP 7 UPPER NORTHWEST

FIELD

RD

▷ 8 ▷

W

DR

RD

AMA RD

WYOMING

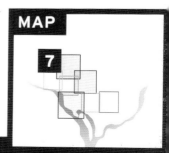

MAP

7

ADAMS MORGAN/ WOODLEY PARK

For young Washington, Adams Morgan is *the* place to be, and 18th Street, winding from Dupont Circle to Columbia Road, is its nerve center. Retro clothing boutiques and fortune-tellers make their home here, sharing sidewalk space with ethnic restaurants from around the world – Ethiopia is especially well represented. After dark, dance clubs open their doors and music pours into the street. This is also the time when street folk come out in full force. For the most part, they're harmless. Still, the area has endured a violent-crime streak since mid-2006, so it's best to enjoy the strip's late-night offerings with a companion in tow.

Just north of Adams Morgan is edgy Mount Pleasant. The area is home to a friendly mix of non-profit types, bohemians, and Latin American immigrants. Here, authentic Salvadoran food is plentiful and gritty dive bars are a refreshing change from the bouncers and steep covers of downtown clubs.

On the other side of Rock Creek Park, the Woodley Park neighborhood brings a homey touch of suburbia to the city. It also enjoys a prime location, with the National Zoo just steps away and Rock Creek Park in its backyard.

MAP

8

⭐ SIGHTS

Best place to witness a political protest:
LINCOLN MEMORIAL, p. 2

Best memorial to see at night:
NATIONAL WORLD WAR II MEMORIAL, p. 3

Most picturesque monument to view from the Tidal Basin:
THOMAS JEFFERSON MEMORIAL, p. 4

Most emotionally charged museum:
UNITED STATES HOLOCAUST MEMORIAL MUSEUM, p. 5

Best spot for personal reflection:
VIETNAM VETERANS MEMORIAL, p. 6

D.C.'s most iconic landmark: **WASHINGTON MONUMENT,** p. 6

Best place to glimpse the president: **THE WHITE HOUSE,** p. 7

Most visited museum on the planet:
NATIONAL AIR AND SPACE MUSEUM, p. 9

Best place to admire U.S. founding documents:
NATIONAL ARCHIVES, p. 10

Best place to get inspired: **NATIONAL GALLERY OF ART,** p. 11

World's largest museum complex:
SMITHSONIAN INSTITUTION, p. 12

Best spot to see justice served: **SUPREME COURT,** p. 13

Best place to see members of Congress in action:
UNITED STATES CAPITOL, p. 14

Most diplomatic street: **EMBASSY ROW,** p. 17

Sight most likely to leave you speechless:
ARLINGTON NATIONAL CEMETERY, p. 19

MAP 1 | **WESTERN MALL/FOGGY BOTTOM**

LINCOLN MEMORIAL

Even if it's your first time, walking up the steps of the Lincoln Memorial feels familiar. That's probably because its image is imprinted on every U.S. penny and $5 bill, and over the years it has become a symbol of freedom and democracy. It was here, in 1963, that Martin Luther King Jr. addressed the nation with his famous "I Have a Dream" speech. The scene of public protests and demonstrations broadcast globally, the Lincoln Memorial is understandably the city's most visited memorial.

Construction on this Greek temple–style structure began in 1914, and Lincoln's only surviving son attended the building's dedication in 1922. The 19-foot statue of the 16th president, designed by Daniel Chester French, is about as lifelike as marble can be, and the seated, brooding figure dominates the interior space. Surrounding it are Lincoln's most famous

CAPITAL-IZING ON HOLLYWOOD

Washington D.C. might be on the other side of the country from Hollywood, but it still basks in the cinematic spotlight from time to time. More movie producers are turning to the nation's capital to set scenes filled with international intrigue, historical grandeur, and political drama (in other words, *The West Wing*). Perhaps Washington's most famous movie marker is the stairway at the 3600 block of Prospect Street, known as ***The Exorcist* stairs (p. 85),** where an ill-fated priest falls to his death in one of the most haunting film scenes of all time. Always evoking sentiment and patriotism, the monuments on the **National Mall (p. 83)** are featured in some of the most iconic American movies. In *Mr. Smith Goes to Washington,* the title character gets inspiration from overhearing a young boy reading aloud from the Gettysburg Address inscription at the **Lincoln Memorial (p. 2),** and Robin Wright Penn fulfills many a child's fantasy of wading, fully clothed, into the Reflecting Pool in *Forrest Gump.* An icon of a different sort figures in *The Pelican Brief:* Denzel Washington meets with Secret Service agents at local landmark **Ben's Chili Bowl (p. 33).**

SIGHTS

LINCOLN MEMORIAL   NATIONAL WORLD WAR II MEMORIAL

words etched in stone: the Gettysburg Address on one wall, his second inaugural address on another.

Packed tour buses flock to this site daily, especially in the spring and summer. If you'd rather not share the moment with a crowd, visit at dusk or early morning. By the light of a full moon, the images in the 2,029-foot-long Reflecting Pool, directly across from the main entrance, are spectacular.

 D2✪38 23RD ST. NW 202-426-6841
WWW.NPS.GOV/LINC
PARK RANGER HOURS: DAILY 8 A.M.–MIDNIGHT;
CLOSED DEC. 25

◖ NATIONAL WORLD WAR II MEMORIAL

Honoring what Tom Brokaw has called the Greatest Generation, the National World War II Memorial opened to the public on April 29, 2004, nearly 60 years after the end of the war.

Nestled between the Washington Monument and the Lincoln Memorial on the National Mall, the site is an ambitious mix of granite and bronze, with a strong circular motif and careful attention to those who played a role during the war. Two flagpoles stand at the ceremonial entrance on 17th Street, and the base of each bears the insignia of every branch of the armed forces that served. Along the raised walkway and steps toward the plaza are 24 bronze bas-relief panels depicting those who supported the war both at home and abroad.

The monument's centerpiece is the Memorial Plaza, which incorporates a revamped Rainbow Pool and quotes from Franklin Delano Roosevelt, Harry Truman, and Dwight Eisenhower, among others. Marking the north and south entrances to the plaza, the Atlantic and Pacific Pavilions commemorate the two theaters of war. Smaller pillars, 56 in all, encircle the plaza and represent each U.S. state and territory at the time of the conflict. A sculpted bronze rope connects the pillars and pavilions, symbolizing the unity of the nation at the time. Other details include the striking, if eerie, backlights for night viewing and the sobering Field of Stars — 4,000 gold stars on the Wall of Freedom representing the more than 400,000 who gave all for their country.

 D5✪40 17TH ST. BTWN. CONSTITUTION AND INDEPENDENCE AVES. NW 202-426-6841
WWW.NPS.GOV/NWWM
PARK RANGER HOURS: DAILY 8 A.M.–MIDNIGHT;
CLOSED DEC. 25TH

◖ THOMAS JEFFERSON MEMORIAL

Thomas Jefferson's contributions to our nation — as a statesman, spiritual leader, independent thinker, and ultimately as president — were immense. He wrote the Declaration of Independence, orchestrated the Louisiana Purchase, and founded the University of Virginia. Fittingly, his memorial overlooking the Tidal Basin is arguably the most graceful and inspirational structure in Washington.

The creation of the Jefferson Memorial had a bumpy start. In 1934, architect John Russell Pope was hired to design the structure. Inspired by Jefferson's own neoclassical architectural tastes, Pope modeled the monument on Rome's Pantheon. However, the Commission of Fine Arts worried that the open, colonnaded structure too closely resembled the Lincoln Memorial. President Franklin D. Roosevelt was asked to intervene; he liked the design and gave his permission to proceed, and in 1939, he laid the cornerstone of the memorial.

Another two years passed before Rudolph Evans was commissioned to sculpt the imperial, bronze statue of Jefferson, which stands 19 feet tall atop a six-foot marble pedestal. Carved into the walls around the statue are excerpts from Jefferson's writings: portions of the Declaration, admonitions against slavery, and statements advocating religious freedom.

The memorial is especially breathtaking in late March and early April, when the famed cherry blossoms are in bloom. At night, energy-efficient lighting illuminates parts of the site, making the after-dark experience at the Jefferson Memorial very rewarding.

 F5✪50 EAST BASIN DR. SW 202-426-6841
WWW.NPS.GOV/THJE
PARK RANGER HOURS: DAILY 8 A.M.–MIDNIGHT;
CLOSED DEC. 25TH

THOMAS JEFFERSON MEMORIAL

UNITED STATES HOLOCAUST
MEMORIAL MUSEUM

◖ UNITED STATES HOLOCAUST MEMORIAL MUSEUM

Dedicated to the mandate that society must never forget the atrocities of World War II, the U.S. Holocaust Memorial Museum opened in 1993 and has since remained one of the most powerful, sobering, and memorable sights in Washington.

Designed by James Ingo Freed of Pei Cobb Freed & Partners, the five-story redbrick-and-limestone building is itself a major part of the experience. Occupying two acres, the huge education and research complex resembles a postmodern penitentiary, with a series of watchtowers along two sides.

Upon entering the permanent exhibit, you receive a photo identity card with personal statistics about an actual victim of the Holocaust; during the visit, you learn more about the identity of the person on your card and at the end of you visit, you learn whether or not the person survived. Using a barrage of documentary films, tapes, and personal artifacts, the permanent exhibit covers three floors, each documenting a different time span from 1933 to present day. The exhaustive archives allow you to track the public's increasing awareness of the tragedy through films and newspaper coverage.

Many of the graphic exhibits are profoundly disturbing and are not recommended for young children. You will not soon forget these images: a roomful of shoes of the victims, an actual train car used to shuttle prisoners to the concentration camps, a white-plaster scale model of a death camp. End your visit in the Hall of Remembrance, an unadorned open space provided for contemplation and commemorative ceremonies, where you can light a candle to honor one of the Holocaust victims.

 D6❂44 100 RAOUL WALLENBERG PL. SW 202-488-0400, 800-400-9373 (TIMED-ENTRY PASSES FOR PERMANENT EXHIBIT HALL) WWW.USHMM.ORG HOURS: DAILY 10 A.M.–5:30 P.M. (SUMMER HOURS VARY); CLOSED ON YOM KIPPUR AND DEC. 25TH

SIGHTS

◖ VIETNAM VETERANS MEMORIAL

Known simply as the Wall, this haunting memorial to those killed or missing in the Vietnam War is a "quiet place, meant for personal reflection and reckoning." Day and night, scores of people come to do just that, paying their respects at the black granite walls etched with more than 58,000 names.

Designed by artist Maya Ying Lin, the two walls rise from grassy earth and meet at a 10-foot peak. To quell the controversy surrounding the starkness of the sculpture, which was seen by many as too abstract, the life-size *Three Servicemen Statue*, depicting young servicemen of different ethnic origins, was placed nearby in 1984, two years after the memorial's dedication. In addition, the Glenna Goodacre-designed Vietnam Women's Memorial, a bronze statue of three military women tending to a fallen soldier, was erected in 1993.

Despite the many visitors, the area around the memorial is very quiet. Many bring charcoal and tracing paper to make rubbings of the names of their loved ones; some also leave behind poignant offerings such as photographs, dog tags, helmets, birthday cards, flowers, and toys.

Beautiful in all seasons and at all times of day, the walls' highly polished surfaces reflect the trees, sky, and flags in vivid color. The scene is most ethereal at night, when city traffic on Constitution Avenue has quieted and the crowds have ebbed.

 C3❂33 HENRY BACON DR. AND CONSTITUTION AVE. NW 202-426-6841 WWW.NPS.GOV/VIVE PARK RANGER HOURS: DAILY 8 A.M.–MIDNIGHT; CLOSED DEC. 25TH

◖ WASHINGTON MONUMENT

Originally conceived as an equestrian statue to honor George Washington, this monument to the Father of Our Country has become the most distinguished icon in our nation's capital.

Made of granite with a marble exterior, the monument reaches 555 feet – the world's tallest masonry struc-

VIETNAM VETERANS MEMORIAL   THE WHITE HOUSE

ture – and weighs 90,854 tons. Construction began in 1848, but political disputes, lack of funds, and the Civil War delayed its completion until 1884 (and it was another four years before it opened to the general public). Because the quarry from which the initial marble was drawn had run out by the time construction resumed after the Civil War, there is a visible color change about a third of the way up, where the Maryland marble meets the Massachusetts marble.

Today, expect to be whisked up to the observation platform via a 60-second elevator ride; eight small windows afford a spectacular view of the city. There was a time when people were permitted to walk up the 898 steps to the summit (today there are 896 steps). In fact, when the elevator first opened, only men were allowed to take it since it was thought to be dangerous, and women received the dubious privilege of what is literally a monumental workout.

Reopened in April 2005, there are now extensive security enhancements in and around the monument. Free tickets for timed entry into the edifice are available at the kiosk on the Washington Monument grounds on a first-come, first-served basis. (Lines are long, and tickets tend to run out quickly, especially in the spring and summer.) Reserved tickets can be ordered between 24 hours and four months in advance and cost $1.50, plus a $.50 handling fee for each order.

 MAP 1 D6✪42 CONSTITUTION AVE. AND 15TH ST. SW 202-426-6841, 800-967-2283 (TICKETS) WWW.NPS.GOV/WAMO HOURS: DAILY 9 A.M.-4:45 P.M.

◖ THE WHITE HOUSE

Visitors are often surprised to find the White House in the heart of Washington's downtown business district surrounded by hotels, restaurants, and museums – and not in a residential neighborhood. Yet, despite its stately Greek Revival architecture and status as a symbol of the federal government, the White House is home to the president and his family.

In 1800, the first resident, John Adams, moved in. Since then, the White House has undergone many changes reflecting the wishes of its occupants: FDR added the East Wing, Harry Truman added a second-story balcony, and Bill Clinton built a custom jogging track.

Anticipated dangers to the commander-in-chief have caused security measures to tighten over the years, and regulations governing access change frequently. Until 1928, Americans could enter the White House every day at noon to meet the president. In 1995, after the Oklahoma City bombing, President Clinton closed to traffic the section of Pennsylvania Avenue in front of the White House. It remains closed today due to security concerns.

The "President's house" isn't completely off-limits, though. Tours for parties of 10 or more can be requested through members of Congress. Requests may be granted six months in advance and are scheduled approximately one month prior. In the summer it's best to make arrangements a few months ahead to be safe. Tours can be scheduled Tuesday–Saturday 7:30 A.M.–12:30 P.M. (except for Federal holidays).

MAP 1 B5✪26 1600 PENNSYLVANIA AVE. NW
202-456-7041   WWW.WHITEHOUSE.GOV

BUREAU OF ENGRAVING AND PRINTING
Inside this imposing, columned government building, blank sheets of paper are transformed into bills worth $1-100, and the tour that walks you through the process is one of the most interesting and popular in Washington.

MAP 1 E6✪48 14TH AND C STS. SW
202-874-2330   WWW.MONEYFACTORY.GOV

SIDE WALKS

Before heading to the White House for a glimpse at a distance, stop for a quick bite at **Bread Line (p. 22).**

After snapping pictures of D.C.'s most executive address, visit the nearby **Corcoran Gallery of Art (p. 66)** to see its amazing collection of American art.

For more American works, walk a few blocks up to the **Renwick Gallery (p. 66)** for decorative-arts exhibits, including a not-to-be-missed display of handmade furniture.

Make your way to the Foggy Bottom-GWU Metro station to catch the free shuttle to Kennedy Center. The **Millennium Stage (p. 76)** puts on performances at 6 P.M. everyday, gratis, and you won't even need a ticket.

CONSTITUTION GARDENS   NATIONAL AIR AND SPACE MUSEUM

CONSTITUTION GARDENS

This 50-acre landscaped park bordering the Reflecting Pool is an idyllic setting for a memorial dedicated to the signers of the U.S. Constitution.

MAP 1 D5✪41   CONSTITUTION AVE. AND 17TH ST. NW
202-426-6841   WWW.NPS.GOV/COGA

FRANKLIN DELANO ROOSEVELT MEMORIAL

This expansive 7.5-acre park is a magnet for tourists. The best time to enjoy the waterfalls, shade trees, and sculptures is at night, without the crowds.

MAP 1 E4✪46   WEST BASIN DR.
202-426-6841   WWW.NPS.GOV/FDRM

KOREAN WAR VETERANS MEMORIAL

Dedicated in 1995, this hillside memorial consists of 19 larger-than-life soldiers sculpted in stainless steel. A granite wall and Pool of Remembrance add to the dramatic setting, as does fiber-optic lighting for night viewing.

MAP 1 D3✪39   INDEPENDENCE AVE. AND DANIEL FRENCH DR. SW
202-426-6841   WWW.NPS.GOV/KWVM

NATIONAL AQUARIUM

The nation's oldest aquarium is inside the Department of Commerce. Feed the piranhas, scare the sharks, or behold any of the other 200 species on display.

MAP 1 B6✪32   14TH ST. AND CONSTITUTION AVE. NW
202-482-2825   WWW.NATIONALAQUARIUM.COM

MAP 2 | SMITHSONIAN/PENN QUARTER

◖ NATIONAL AIR AND SPACE MUSEUM

From the original 1903 Wright Brothers flyer to the *Apollo 11* command module, the National Air and Space Museum holds the world's largest collection of aircraft and spacecraft. With the original location on the Mall only able to contain 10 percent of its objects, NASM opened the Steven F. Udvar-Hazy Center in late 2003.

At the museum on the Mall – a Washington landmark since 1976 – you'll find one gallery that encompasses the "Milestones of Flight" exhibition and more than 20 other galleries, including the hands-on "How Things Fly." Check out the exhibit celebrating the flight at Kitty Hawk. There's also the Lockheed Martin IMAX Theater, whose premiere film, *To Fly,* imparts the sensation of flying in a hot air balloon, a variety of airplanes, and, finally, a spacecraft.

The Udvar-Hazy Center is the larger of the two sites, by far. Located in nearby Chantilly, Virginia, the center will eventually contain nearly 80 percent of the museum's holdings, including 127 aircraft and 143 space artifacts.

With millions of visitors annually, NASM is the most visited Smithsonian museum, so crowds are always a part of the experience. However, they tend to recede in late afternoon and during the winter months.

MAP 2 E5✪54 INDEPENDENCE AVE. AND 4TH ST. SW 202-633-1000
WWW.NASM.SI.EDU
HOURS: DAILY 10 A.M.–5:30 P.M. (SUMMER HOURS VARY);
CLOSED DEC. 25TH

◖ NATIONAL ARCHIVES

The National Archives and Records Administration building first opened in 1935, but the venerable institution has since grown to include the National Archives at College Park, Maryland, as well as 19 regional record facilities and 11 presidential libraries spread out across the United States. In Washington alone, NARA houses more than six billion pieces of paper and 11 million pictures.

The main attraction of the neoclassical National Archives building on Pennsylvania Avenue is the Rotunda for the Charters of Freedom. Reopened in 2003 after a three-year renovation, this exhibition space features a new-and-improved display

SIDE WALKS

After viewing the United States' important historical documents at the National Archives, it's just a quick walk up 7th to reach energetic Penn Quarter. Stop in at **Apartment Zero (p. 52)** to browse the chic selection of home furnishings.

Check out the menus hanging in restaurant windows until you find somewhere you'd like to eat. You have plenty of options: popular eateries like **Jaleo (p. 25), Café Atlántico (p. 23),** and **Zengo D.C. (p. 26)** are all located in this area.

During your inevitable wait for a table, pop over to **Woolly Mammoth Theatre (p. 78)** to pick up tickets for a performance – if you're lucky, you might be able to score a couple deep-discount stampede seats.

After the show, get drinks at **Poste (p. 43).**

SIGHTS

NATIONAL ARCHIVES   NATIONAL GALLERY OF ART

of the Declaration of Independence, the Constitution (all four pages, a first), and the Bill of Rights. The National Archives Experience, a continuing program, includes a Special Exhibition Gallery with document-based exhibits of current affairs.

Other spaces of interest in the National Archives are the five Public Vaults, with exhibition spaces thematically connected to the Preamble to the Constitution, and the 290-seat William G. McGowan Theater. By day the theater runs a film illustrating the relationship between public records and the democratic process. At night it becomes a showcase for documentaries, as well as a gathering place for citizens to discuss issues of the day.

MAP 2 D4 ✪ 44   CONSTITUTION AVE. BTWN. 7TH AND 9TH STS. NW
866-272-6272
WWW.ARCHIVES.GOV/DC-METRO/WASHINGTON
ROTUNDA AND EXHIBIT HALL HOURS: MAR. 15–LABOR DAY
DAILY 10 A.M.–7 P.M.; LABOR DAY–MAR. 14 DAILY 10 A.M.–
5:30 PM. (CLOSED THANKSGIVING DAY AND DEC. 25)

⬥ NATIONAL GALLERY OF ART

The National Gallery of Art was founded by financier and art collector Andrew W. Mellon. His endowment included 126 paintings, with 21 masterpieces from the Hermitage, and his sculpture collection. Other benefactors followed suit, and within 30 years the collection outgrew the original building, leading to the addition of another building in 1978. Today, the West and East Buildings contain collections from the Middle Ages to the present.

With a domed rotunda over a marble-colonnaded fountain, the West Building is a neoclassical masterpiece. More than 1,000 works on permanent display include paintings by Van Gogh, Rembrandt, El Greco, da Vinci, and Vermeer. You'll also find one of the world's finest Impressionist collections. In contrast, the East Building, designed by the architecture firm of I. M. Pei, is an ultra-modern palace of glass walls and jutting angles filled with works by 20th-century masters such as Picasso, Modigliani, Matisse, Pollock, and Rothko. The art displays continue outside, where the Sculpture Garden spreads over two city blocks and includes items by Joan Miró, Roy Lichtenstein, and Ellsworth Kelly. Year-round café service and a central fountain make it a delightful luncheon spot.

If you're susceptible to art overload, make your first stop the West Building's Micro Gallery, where you can design a personalized tour. The gallery also offers other programs such as film series and – September–June – Sunday-evening concerts.

MAP 2 D5 ❹46 CONSTITUTION AVE. NW BTWN. 4TH AND 7TH STS. NW
202-737-4215   WWW.NGA.GOV
HOURS: MON.-SAT. 10 A.M.-5 P.M., SUN. 11 A.M.-6 P.M.

◖ SMITHSONIAN INSTITUTION

Founded in 1846, the Smithsonian grew out of a bequest left by English scientist James Smithson, who specified that his money be used "to found...: an estab-lishment for the increase and diffusion of knowledge." His wish was carried out. With 19 museums and gal-leries, among them the National Zoological Park, the yet-to-open National Museum of African American Culture and History Museum, and nine research facili-ties around the world containing more than 143 mil-lion artifacts, the Smithsonian is the world's largest museum complex.

The museum got its start in the turreted red sand-stone building known as "the Castle." A fanciful com-bination of Romanesque revival and early Gothic architecture, the Castle has retained its look despite several major renovations.

The state-of-the-art information center is the requisite first stop. The center provides an 18-minute film giving an overview of the Institution, interactive computer touch-screens dispensing information in six languages, and a scale model of Washington's downtown area. Electronic wall maps highlight popular attractions, and information specialists are on hand to answer questions concerning the Smithsonian's lectures, concerts, festivals,and tours.

Many of the Smithsonian's most popular museums, including the National Air and Space Museum and the Freer and Sackler Galleries, are just steps away from the Castle. Visit-worthy for the sheer quality and quantity of the collections, the Smithsonian museums have the added appeal of free admission.

 E3 ⊕49   1000 JEFFERSON DR. SW 202-633-1000
WWW.SI.EDU
MUSEUM HOURS: DAILY 10 A.M.–5:30 P.M.INFORMATION
CENTER HOURS: DAILY 8:30 A.M.–5:30 P.M.

THE OLD POST OFFICE PAVILION
Home to the Bells of Congress, this is Washington's first sky-scraper. The bells are rung only for special occasions, but the real draw is the vantage from the observation deck of the clock tower: the view includes the downtown skyline and the Mall.

MAP 2 C2 ⊕29   1100 PENNSYLVANIA AVE. NW
202-289-4224   WWW.OLDPOSTOFFICEDC.COM

MAP 3 | CAPITOL HILL

⬕ SUPREME COURT

The nation's highest court led a nomadic life for 145 years, with the justices meeting at times in New York City, Philadelphia, private homes, and taverns. Finally, in 1929, Chief Justice William Howard Taft (the only president ever to serve on the Court) convinced Congress to allocate funds for a Supreme Court building.

Located on the grounds of a former Civil War prison, the weighty neoclassical structure was designed by architect Cass Gilbert to symbolize the importance of the independent branch of government that it houses. Two massive figures representing the Contemplation of Justice and the Guardian or Authority of Law flank a broad staircase that leads up to 16 Corinthian columns. Sculpted bronze entry doors open into the Great Hall, where busts of former chief justices are set on marble pedestals.

In addition to impressive architecture, a visit to the

SIDE WALKS

Unless you're a law buff, a visit to the Supreme Court may not involve much more than a photo-op. But the surrounding Capitol Hill neighborhood offers many distractions.

Since you're so close, don't miss the **Library of Congress (p. 15).** A look at the beautiful building is reason enough, to say nothing of its vast stores of information.

Pennsylvania Avenue hosts a cluster of retail activity that's worth a look. Try **Pulp on the Hill (p. 54)** for gag gifts and unique greeting cards.

Head east toward Eastern Market, which is best on weekends. Find heat in a bottle at **Uncle Brutha's Hot Sauce Emporium (p. 55).**

Finish your jaunt with a bite to eat at **Montmartre (p. 27),** a bistro that evokes its eponymous Parisian neighborhood.

13

UNITED STATES CAPITOL   UNION STATION

Supreme Court can offer a chance to sit in on a session. The Court hears oral arguments at 10 A.M. Monday–Wednesday, starting the first Monday of October and continuing every two weeks until late April. (The Court then continues to sit through the end of June, issuing orders and opinions.) All told, the Court decides about 100 cases of national importance a year. Reservations are not required to hear oral arguments, which are open to the public on a first-come, first-served basis. You can choose to stay for an entire argument or a brief visit. On days when the Court is not sitting, the staff often presents lectures every hour on the half hour 9:30 A.M.–3:30 P.M.

MAP 3 **D4❂12** 1 1ST ST. NE 202-479-3211
WWW.SUPREMECOURTUS.GOV
HOURS: MON.-FRI. 9 A.M.-4:30 P.M.
(EXCEPT FEDERAL HOLIDAYS)

◖ UNITED STATES CAPITOL

Pierre-Charles L'Enfant described Jenkins Hill as "a pedestal waiting for a monument." With its enormous cast-iron dome, Roman pillars, and ornate fountains, the U.S. Capitol building certainly qualifies. Sweeping lawns and flowering gardens, designed by Frederick Law Olmsted of New York's Central Park fame, enhance the neoclassical structure's beauty.

History permeates the four-acre complex, where Congress crafts laws as it has since John Adams addressed its first session in 1800. Over the years, the Capitol has been burned (during the War of 1812), rebuilt, and restored, all the while enduring as a symbol of democracy.

Appropriately, the bronze *Statue of Freedom* tops the 285-foot dome. Inside, a frieze around the rim re-creates 400 years of history. The *Apotheosis of Washington*, an allegorical fresco by the same artist, fills the eye of the dome, while immense oil paintings by John Trumbull depict scenes from the American Revolution. Guided tours are available by obtaining a free timed-entry pass from a kiosk located near 1st Street and Independence Avenue SW.

 MAP 3 **D2✪11** BTWN. CONSTITUTION AVE., INDEPENDENCE AVE.,
AND 1ST ST. 202-225-6827
WWW.AOC.GOV
HOURS: MON.-SAT. 9 A.M.-4:30 P.M.;
CLOSED THANKSGIVING DAY AND DEC. 25TH

LIBRARY OF CONGRESS

With its sweeping stairways and columned halls, the Library of Congress is visually and architecturally stunning. It's almost a footnote to say that it contains the world's most comprehensive collection of human creativity and knowledge.

MAP 3 **E4✪16** THOMAS JEFFERSON BUILDING, 101 INDEPENDENCE AVE. SE
202-707-8000   WWW.LOC.GOV

NATIONAL JAPANESE AMERICAN MEMORIAL

The inscriptions at this triangular plaza commemorate Japanese American patriotism during World War II. A statue depicting two cranes bound with barbed wire symbolizes the battle to overcome prejudice.

MAP 3 **C2✪10** LOUISIANA AVE. BTWN. NEW JERSEY AVE. AND D ST. NW
202-530-0015   WWW.NJAMF.COM

UNION STATION

At one time the world's largest train station, Union Station, with its Beaux-Arts-style architecture, marble floors, and high coffered ceilings, is gorgeous and practical as a destination for transit, shops, and restaurants.

MAP 3 **B3✪4** 50 MASSACHUSETTS AVE. NE
202-289-1908   WWW.UNIONSTATIONDC.COM

UNITED STATES BOTANIC GARDEN

First established in 1820, the nation's oldest continually operating botanic garden boasts an old world desert, numerous varieties of orchids, and – the highlight – a tropical rainforest of towering palms and steamy pools.

MAP 3 **E1✪14** 100 MARYLAND AVE. SW
202-225-8333   WWW.USBG.GOV

MAP 4 GEORGETOWN

COX'S ROW

Colonel John Cox – the first elected mayor of Georgetown – built these five elegant Federal-style houses in 1815, and today they offer a postcard view of the neighborhood.

MAP 4 **E3✪14** 3337-3339 N ST. NW

SIGHTS

UNITED STATES
BOTANIC GARDEN

EMBASSY ROW

GEORGETOWN UNIVERSITY

Georgetown is not only the country's oldest Catholic and
Jesuit university, but is also one of its most beautiful and
exclusive. Healy Hall's gothic spires are striking even from
the other side of the Potomac.

MAP 4 D1 **◆9** 37TH AND O STS. NW
202-687-0100 WWW.GEORGETOWN.EDU

OAK HILL CEMETERY

Established in 1848, this enchanting garden cemetery situated on 25 hilly acres boasts exceptional statuary and a
James Renwick-designed Gothic-revival chapel. No pictures
allowed on the grounds.

MAP 4 B6 **◆6** 3001 R ST. NW
202-337-2835
WWW.CR.NPS.GOV/NR/TRAVEL/WASH/DC9.HTM

TUDOR PLACE HISTORIC HOUSE AND GARDEN

The former home of Martha Washington's granddaughter,
Martha Custis Peter, this brick mansion is filled with exquisite
artifacts of the Peter family. Unwind in five-acres of meticu-
lously designed gardens that are known for boxwood and the
Japanese Tea House.

MAP 4 C4 **◆8** 1644 31ST ST. NW
202-965-0400 WWW.TUDORPLACE.ORG

MAP 5 DUPONT CIRCLE

THE BREWMASTER'S CASTLE

Striking a remarkable contrast to its cosmopolitan Dupont
Circle surrounds, this venerable edifice is the most intact
late-Victorian home in the country. It's the former home of
Christian Heurich, who still holds the title of "world's oldest brewer" since he operated his brewery until he died at
age 102.

MAP 5 C5 **◆34** 1307 NEW HAMPSHIRE AVE. NW
202-429-1894 WWW.HEURICHHOUSE.ORG

MAP 6 | 14TH AND U

AFRICAN AMERICAN CIVIL WAR MEMORIAL

Unveiled in 1998 to honor black troops' contribution to the Civil War, this memorial, located just outside the U Street Metro station, includes a sculpture of black soldiers leaving for the war as its centerpiece.

MAP 6 A4✪17 1200 U ST. NW
202-667-2667   WWW.AFROAMCIVILWAR.ORG

FRANKLIN SQUARE

When Alexander Graham Bell transmitted the first wireless message from here in 1880, this downtown park was considered "the country." The adjoining Franklin School, opened in 1868, is the only building from that era still standing in the square.

MAP 6 F4✪58 14TH AND K STS. NW
WWW.CR.NPS.GOV/NR/TRAVEL/WASH/DC29.HTM

THIRD CHURCH OF CHRIST, SCIENTIST

Architecture buffs won't want to miss this striking I. M. Pei-designed church, which incorporates his characteristic geometric angles.

MAP 6 F2✪52 900 16TH ST. NW
202-833-3325
HTTP://3RDCHRISTIANSCIENCEDC.COM

MAP 7 | UPPER NORTHWEST

◖ EMBASSY ROW

A few memorable hours can be well spent by strolling along Embassy Row. More than 50 countries are represented in this two-mile stretch of Massachusetts Avenue, along with stately private homes, a charming pocket-sized park, and the city's largest mosque.

Beginning with its national flag, each embassy proudly displays its unique character. The Brazilian Embassy is an ultramodern, understated glass box. The Korean Embassy boasts a fountain featuring silver globes poised atop poles. The imposing Chancery of the Italian Embassy, on Whitehaven Street, was completed in 1999; its facade is made from stones cut to size in Italy and shipped to the United States for installation by Italian masons. The four-acre British Embassy, considered the star of Embassy Row, is housed in a magnificent redbrick residence

UNITED STATES NAVAL OBSERVATORY

WASHINGTON NATIONAL CATHEDRAL

built in 1928. A statue of Winston Churchill stands out front, with one foot on British soil – embassy grounds are technically property of that country – and the other on U.S. soil, as a symbol of his Anglo-American descent.

Just east of Rock Creek Park is the operational mosque at the Islamic Center. Visitors are welcome but proper dress is required: Arms and legs must be covered, shoes must be removed, and women must wear a head covering.

While embassies are usually open for official business only, a phone call in advance of your visit may yield different results.

MAP 7 E5✪19 MASSACHUSETTS AVE. NW BTWN. OBSERVATORY CIRCLE AND 15TH ST. NW
WWW.EMBASSY.ORG/EMBASSY_ROW

UNITED STATES NAVAL OBSERVATORY

Stroll the gated perimeter for a peek at the Victorian mansion that has served as the vice president's home since 1977, when Walter Mondale moved in during the Carter administration.

MAP 7 E4✪18 3450 MASSACHUSETTS AVE. NW
202-762-1467   WWW.USNO.NAVY.MIL

WASHINGTON NATIONAL CATHEDRAL

This beautiful Episcopal church's central tower rises 676 feet above sea level and forms D.C.'s highest point. Bring binoculars to appreciate the flying buttresses' quirky gargoyles and grotesques – and the Darth Vader that sits atop the northwest tower.

MAP 7 C3✪16 WISCONSIN AND MASSACHUSETTS AVES. NW
202-537-6200   WWW.CATHEDRAL.ORG

MAP 8 | ADAMS MORGAN/WOODLEY PARK

NATIONAL ZOOLOGICAL PARK

Home to sea lions, tamarin monkeys, giant pandas, tigers, and more, the National Zoo is a sprawling 163 acres with more than 2,400 inhabitants and 400 species.

 A2✪1   3001 CONNECTICUT AVE. NW
202-633-4800
HTTP://NATIONALZOO.SI.EDU

OVERVIEW MAP AND OFF MAP

◖ ARLINGTON NATIONAL CEMETERY

A visit to Arlington National Cemetery is an emotionally charged experience. An average of more than 20 funeral services are performed each day, amounting to 6,400 burials a year. Even if you don't personally know one of the 300,000 buried here, you'll invariably feel a lump in your throat and an overwhelming rush of patriotism looking out over the 612 acres of seemingly endless rows of white headstones.

One of the cemetery's most crowded sights is the gravesite of President John F. Kennedy, marked with the Eternal Flame. Another moving monument is the Tomb of the Unknowns, a grave honoring the unknown soldiers of both World Wars and the Korean War. Tomb Guard Sentinels from the 3rd U.S. Infantry, the oldest active-duty unit in the Army, stand guard here 365 days a year, and the changing of the guard should not be missed.

Other points of interest include Arlington House, the restored former home of Mary Custis and her husband, Robert E. Lee; the Women in Military Service for America Memorial; a memorial commemorating the astronauts killed in the space shuttle *Challenger* and *Columbia* disasters; and Section 27, where more than 3,800 former slaves are buried.

A network of paved roads and steps covers the cemetery's often-steep terrain, and navigating the grounds involves much walking. Cars are permitted only for the disabled or relatives of persons buried here.

OVERVIEW MAP **E2**   VIRGINIA SIDE OF ARLINGTON MEMORIAL BRIDGE
703-607-8000
WWW.ARLINGTONCEMETERY.ORG
HOURS: APR.-SEPT. DAILY 8 A.M.-7 P.M.;
OCT.-MAR. DAILY 8 A.M.-5 P.M.

UNITED STATES MARINE CORPS WAR MEMORIAL

Also known as the Iwo Jima Memorial, this immense sculpture – based on a Pulitzer Prize-winning photograph – honors all marines who died during military duty.

OVERVIEW MAP **D2**   N. MEADE ST. AND MARSHALL DR. IN ARLINGTON, VA
703-289-2500   WWW.NPS.GOV/GWMP/USMC.HTM

UNITED STATES NATIONAL ARBORETUM

Seek refuge in 446 acres of exotic collections that include bonsais, azaleas, and even a fragrance garden. Or tour the sprawling grounds at night on a guided five-mile Full Moon Hike.

OFF MAP   3501 NEW YORK AVE. NE
202-245-2726   WWW.USNA.USDA.GOV

R RESTAURANTS

Hottest restaurant of the moment: **KOMI,** p. 35

Best excuse to break your diet:
MINIBAR RESTAURANT AT CAFÉ ATLÁNTICO, p. 25

Best place for celeb-spotting: **CAFÉ MILANO,** p. 28

Best spot for a clandestine meeting: **BAR PILAR,** p. 33

Most local flavor: **BEN'S CHILI BOWL,** p. 34

Best pizza: **PIZZERIA PARADISO,** p. 32

Best vegetarian fare: **VEGETATE,** p. 36

Best view: **PERRY'S,** p. 39

Best splurge: **CITYZEN,** p. 40

Best chance to overhear political gossip:
OLD EBBITT GRILL, p. 23

PRICE KEY

$ ENTRÉES UNDER $10

$$ ENTRÉES $10-20

$$$ ENTRÉES OVER $20

MAP 1 | WESTERN MALL/FOGGY BOTTOM

BREAD LINE *CAFÉ $*

Just steps from the White House, Bread Line, with its frantic pace and disorderly interior, plays host to Washington's premiere power breakfasts. Spot your favorite spin doctors behind the pages of the *Washington Post* as you sip fresh orange juice or grab a quick croissant.

MAP 1 A5 ® 11   1751 PENNSYLVANIA AVE. NW
202-822-8900

EQUINOX *HOT SPOTS • AMERICAN $$$*

Chef and owner Todd Gray has created a unique restaurant with a front garden room that complements the dressier interior seating. Its proximity to the White House means big names lunch and dine here, enjoying inventive American cooking such as the spiced Virginia hanger steak with braised kale.

MAP 1 A5 ® 9   818 CONNECTICUT AVE. NW
202-331-8118 WWW.EQUINOXRESTAURANT.COM

KINKEAD'S *BUSINESS • SEAFOOD $$$*

Longtime favorite Kinkead's continues to deliver such seafood standards as bouillabaisse and rockfish, plus New England–style dishes like lobster rolls with fries. The wood-and-brass decor

RESTAURANTS

EXECUTIVE ORDERS

In Washington, executive privilege naturally trickles down to cuisine. President Bush can't get enough Southwestern spice, a tip of the cowboy hat to Texas. He's been spotted at raucous **Cactus Cantina (p. 37)** – giving a boost to the city's favorite Tex-Mex joint. (He's rumored to enjoy cheese enchiladas while dining on Pennsylvania Avenue, too.) While Bill Clinton was in office, the city saw a rise of barbecue restaurants, although most have since closed. Despite his famous love of fast food, Clinton also enjoyed curries and counted the lavish Bombay Club (815 Connecticut Ave. NW, 202-659-3727) as a preferred haunt, and it's still a power-broker favorite. And many of D.C.'s working folk who go for drinks after a tough day should thank John F. Kennedy: During Camelot, Kennedy signed a bill legalizing liquor at bars, not just at tables. The saloon at **Clyde's (p. 28)** promptly opened its doors and continues to pull in the crowds. Finally, for a true taste of history, make tracks to the **Old Ebbitt Grill (p. 23),** a presidential palate-pleaser since the first Johnson administration that's steps from the White House dining room.

BREAD LINE   EQUINOX   OLD EBBITT GRILL

and solicitous service (if you're a somebody) sets the clientele of
expense-accounters and politicos at ease.

MAP 1 A4 **R** 6   2000 PENNSYLVANIA AVE. NW
202-296-7700   WWW.KINKEAD.COM

NOTTI BIANCHE   *ROMANTIC • ITALIAN*   *$$*
This cozy Italian trattoria earns raves from romantics and foodies
alike. Spend an intimate evening lingering over roasted poussin
or lamb leg steak, or snack on risotto fritters before a show at
the nearby Kennedy Center – the pre- and post-theater menus
deserve applause.

MAP 1 A2 **R** 2   824 NEW HAMPSHIRE AVE. NW
202-298-8085   WWW.NOTTIBIANCHE.COM

🌙 OLD EBBITT GRILL   *AFTER HOURS • AMERICAN*   *$$*
From its breakfast pancakes to its dinnertime lamb steaks and pork
chops, the Old Ebbitt serves up abundant American fare, making
this buzzing place one of D.C.'s favorite haunts. Finding seating can
be a challenge if you don't have a reservation. The oyster bar, where
fresh bivalves are brought in daily, is always especially crowded.

MAP 1 A6 **R** 16   675 15TH ST. NW
202-347-4800   WWW.EBBITT.COM

ROOF TERRACE RESTAURANT
& BAR   *BUSINESS • NEW AMERICAN*   *$$$*
Inside the Kennedy Center, this glam restaurant affords its
patrons a dazzling view of the Potomac River. The staid chandeliers have been replaced with shiny glass columns and the modern
American menu has been kicked up a notch, with short ribs, duck
breast, and tasty crab cakes.

MAP 1 B1 **R** 17   KENNEDY CENTER, 2700 F ST. NW
202-416-8555   WWW.KENNEDY-CENTER.ORG

MAP 2 SMITHSONIAN/PENN QUARTER

CAFÉ ATLÁNTICO   *HOT SPOTS • NUEVO LATINO*   *$$$*
Topping the favorites lists of most D.C. gourmands, Café Atlántico
is a lively tri-level restaurant serving unbeatable Latin-tinged

JALEO

THE OCEANAIRE SEAFOOD ROOM

fare. Addictive guacamole and a luscious dim sum-style brunch, featuring small plates such as seared watermelon and scallops in orange oil, draw well-heeled crowds.

MAP 2 C4 R37 405 8TH ST. NW
202-393-0812 WWW.CAFEATLANTICO.COM

THE CAUCUS ROOM *BUSINESS • AMERICAN* $$$

D.C. power brokers and other highbrows cozy up to the elegant bar at the posh Caucus Room. Pampered patrons enjoy steak or Maryland crab cakes with a selection from the wine list, but they save room for the kitchen's lavish desserts, such as the coconut cake.

MAP 2 C4 R36 401 9TH ST. NW
202-393-1300 WWW.THECAUCUSROOM.COM

CEIBA *BUSINESS • LATIN AMERICAN* $$$

Latin American cuisine, intoxicating drinks, and a lively open kitchen make Ceiba a downtown favorite. A tangy array of ceviches, fiery duck empanadas, and tender braised pork offer an introduction to the flavors of Brazil, Cuba, Peru, and the Yucatán.

MAP 2 A1 R1 701 14TH ST. NW
202-393-3983 WWW.CEIBARESTAURANT.COM

ELLA'S WOOD FIRED PIZZA *QUICK BITES • PIZZA/ITALIAN* $$

Don't let the staid office facade fool you – Ella's is one of the finest pizzerias in town. Tourists and locals choose from a laundry list of delicious pies topped with everything from pine nuts to shrimp. A fine array of salads, pastas, and a respectable antipasto platter rounds out the menu. It's a steal at happy hour, when the chefs offer up free pies.

MAP 2 B4 R19 901 F ST. NW
202-638-3434

FOGO DE CHAO *BUSINESS • BRAZILIAN* $$$

Meats on swords are the order of the day at this flashy Brazilian *churrascaria* that combines showmanship with sizzle. Enjoy servings of 15 different cuts of fire-roasted meats served with traditional sides such as fried bananas. Vegetarians, rejoice: There's also a massive salad bar.

MAP 2 C3 R30 1101 PENNSYLVANIA AVE. NW
202-347-4668 WWW.FOGODECHAO.COM

FULL KEE *AFTER HOURS • CHINESE* $$

Soup pots simmer alongside hanging ducks in the window of this Chinatown eatery that's open until 1 A.M. on weekends. If you're feeling bold, ask the chef to prepare his favorite, though you can't go wrong with Hong Kong Noodles. Be forewarned: The specials are written in Chinese.

MAP 2 A5 **R7** 509 H ST. NW
202-371-2233

INDEBLEU *AFTER HOURS • FUSION* $$$

IndeBleu bills itself as an "experience," and it delivers on the hype with exotic, sinfully delicious entrées, such as the standout foie gras sandwich with rose petal marmalade, and bracing, naughtily named drinks (try the Ménage à Trois of apples or the orange-and-banana Cheeky Monkey).

MAP 2 A4 **R5** 707 G ST. NW
202-333-2538 WWW.BLEU.COM/INDEBLEU

JALEO *HOT SPOTS • SPANISH* $$

Still the most popular source for Spanish tapas in D.C., this corner eatery delights all comers with its tasteful meals and lively ambience. Chicken, mussels, sweet peppers, and potatoes are transformed into a variety of savory hot and cold dishes that pair well with crusty breads and an abundant wine selection.

MAP 2 B4 **R24** 480 7TH ST. NW
202-628-7949 WWW.JALEO.COM

LE PARADOU *BUSINESS • FRENCH* $$$

Rich sauces, rich wines, and rich patrons are the hallmarks of this Penn Quarter showplace. The service is polished, the setting lavish – ideal for a decadent night out or that crucial business lunch. Grazers (and budget-minded gourmets) will love the new small-plate menu featuring delicacies such as lobster risotto and osetra caviar.

MAP 2 C4 **R41** 678 INDIANA AVE. NW
202-347-6780 WWW.LEPARADOU.NET

◖ MINIBAR RESTAURANT AT CAFÉ ATLÁNTICO *HOT SPOTS • NUEVO LATINO* $$$

At this six-person counter within Café Atlántico, an innovative prix-fixe tasting menu takes guests on a culinary roller coaster. Brace yourself for some unusual combos; with dishes like foie gras "cotton candy," this isn't for the faint of heart.

MAP 2 C4 **R38** 405 8TH ST. NW
202-393-0812 (SPECIFY MINIBAR WHEN MAKING
RESERVATIONS) WWW.CAFEATLANTICO.COM

THE OCEANAIRE SEAFOOD ROOM *BUSINESS • SEAFOOD* $$$

Evocative of the 1930s, this luxury seafood restaurant believes that more is more, and features the freshest catches served in mammoth portions. D.C. power players and city folk come for the fine service and first-rate dishes, including fresh oysters, grilled fish, seafood soups, and heavenly key lime pie.

MAP 2 B2 **R9** 1201 F ST. NW
202-347-2277 WWW.OCEANAIRESEAFOODROOM.COM

OYA *HOT SPOTS • AMERICAN $$$*

If the *Sex in the City* foursome came to D.C., you'd find them at Oya. Sleek and playful, with more mirrors than a funhouse, Oya draws a hip crowd who expect to pay big bucks for their striped bass, turbot, and colorful cocktails.

MAP 2 A4 **R2** 777 9TH ST. NW
202-393-1400 WWW.OYADC.COM

RASIKA *BUSINESS • INDIAN $$$*

Rasika is Sanskrit for "flavors," and there are plenty of them here. The glowing dining room is awash in red and orange, and the food is equally colorful: scallops brightened with a tingling red pepper sauce, a deep amber vindaloo that's complex without being overpowering. Oenophiles take note: Rasika is renowned for its wine list.

MAP 2 C5 **R42** 633 D ST. NW
202-637-1222 WWW.RASIKARESTAURANT.COM

RED SAGE *BUSINESS • SOUTHWESTERN $$$*

The casual upstairs café elevates Southwestern cooking to new heights, with flavor-packed chilis and colorful entrées. In the dressier downstairs dining room, dramatic presentations of duck, tuna, lamb, and chicken blend the sunny flavors of the Mediterranean and American West while vying for center stage with fanciful cowboy decor.

MAP 2 B1 **R8** 605 14TH ST. NW
202-638-4444 WWW.REDSAGE.COM

TOSCA *BUSINESS • ITALIAN $$$*

Northern Italian delicacies, served à la carte or as a tasting menu, are the specialty here. The dining room resembles an airport lounge, and dishes such as the crabmeat lasagna with creamy sea urchin sauce will make your taste buds take flight.

MAP 2 B3 **R14** 1112 F ST. NW
202-367-1990 WWW.TOSCADC.COM

ZAYTINYA *HOT SPOTS • MEDITERRANEAN $$*

Crowds flock to this stylish mecca of Greek and Turkish mezze, a gift from Jaleo-mastermind chef Jose Andres. Though the no-reservations-after-6:30 P.M. policy ensures that you'll spend time at the bar, a nibble of the light-as-air apricot fritters makes the wait – and the scattered service – worthwhile.

MAP 2 A4 **R4** 701 9TH ST. NW
202-638-0800 WWW.ZAYTINYA.COM

ZENGO D.C. *HOT SPOTS • FUSION $$$*

This two-story temple of tang electrifies the Penn Quarter with a daring menu, potent cocktails, and a lush lounge. Zengo is Japanese for "give and take," and the freewheeling cuisine encourages diners to do just that. The menu skips across Japan and Mexico, from sushi to tacos, all sized for sharing.

MAP 2 A4 **R3** 781 7TH ST. NW
202-393-2929 WWW.MODERNMEXICAN.COM

MAP 3 | CAPITOL HILL

CHARLIE PALMER STEAK *BUSINESS • AMERICAN* $$$
With a rooftop terrace that affords amazing Capitol views, this flashy monument to meat is another jewel in chef Charlie Palmer's crown. The steaks are impossibly thick, and surf is given just as much attention as turf (try the Chesapeake blue crab).

MAP 3 D1 **R** 8   101 CONSTITUTION AVE. NW
202-547-8100   WWW.CHARLIEPALMER.COM

JOHNNY'S HALF SHELL *ROMANTIC • SEAFOOD* $$
Located across from Union Station in new-in-2006 digs, Johnny's Half Shell dishes out a frequently updated menu of marvelous sea-food, including shrimp and grits, grilled squid, and little necks. The elegant simplicity of its offerings matches the high-class surround-ings–marble topped bar, tiled floor, and white-jacketed waitstaff.

MAP 3 B2 **R** 3   400 N. CAPITOL ST.
202-737-0400   WWW.JOHNNYSHALFSHELL.COM

MARKET LUNCH *QUICK BITES • SOUTHERN* $
Even senators wait in line for these legendary grits and crab cakes. Shout your order at the counter, then scramble for a stool at the long, narrow table. Diners are urged not to dawdle over coffee (those who do will be scolded by the staff). Note: The famous blue-berry pancakes are served before noon on Saturdays only.

MAP 3 E6 **R** 29   225 7TH ST. SE
202-547-8444

MONTMARTRE *ROMANTIC • FRENCH* $$
Montmartre adds Parisian je ne sais quoi to the bohemian Eastern Market. Rich French dishes such as braised rabbit leg on a bed of creamy pasta draw artists, families, and even the occasional politician. In the summer months, the patio is refreshing after a morning of haggling with market vendors.

MAP 3 F6 **R** 36   327 7TH ST. SE
202-544-1244

SONOMA *ROMANTIC • NEW AMERICAN* $$
Bright and airy, Sonoma is a dignified place to sample wine by the glass (or taste) and nibble shareable snacks such as charcute-rie, cheese plates, and pizzas. A complete dinner menu entices patrons to discover the perfect varietal to pair with rabbit, boar, or sturgeon.

MAP 3 E4 **R** 21   223 PENNSYLVANIA AVE. SE
202-544-8088   WWW.SONOMADC.COM

MAP 4 | GEORGETOWN

AGRARIA *HOT SPOTS • AMERICAN* $$$
Featuring fresh seafood, steaks, and pasta, the "agrarian" fare at this 2006 newcomer is produced entirely by U.S. family farmers.

The food may be from the American heartland, but the lovely Washington Harbor view – and affluent clientele – is pure Georgetown.

MAP 4 F5 **R43** 3000 K ST. NW
202-298-0003 WWW.AGRARIARESTAURANT.COM

BISTRO FRANÇAIS *AFTER HOURS • FRENCH $$$*
With its brash waiters, garrulous patrons, and mile-long menu that includes the classic cheese-encrusted onion soup, Bistro Français is a slice of Paris on M Street. A popular hangout for D.C. denizens, Bistro Français stays open into the wee hours: 4 A.M. on weekends and 3 A.M. on weekdays.

MAP 4 E5 **R32** 3124-3128 M ST. NW
202-338-3830 WWW.BISTROFRANCAISDC.COM

CAFÉ MILANO *AFTER HOURS • ITALIAN $$$*
Frequented by journalists, politicians, and entertainers, Café Milano offers pretty food for pretty people. Be sure to bring plastic and stick with what's safe on the northern Italian menu – usually pizza and salad. Celeb-sightings on the glamorous outdoor patio compensate for the sometimes-iffy cuisine that can look better than it tastes. Open until 1 A.M. Wednesday–Saturday.

MAP 4 E4 **R20** 3251 PROSPECT ST. NW
202-333-6183 WWW.CAFEMILANODC.COM

CHEZ MAMA-SAN *ROMANTIC • JAPANESE $$*
Home cooking goes East at this tranquil haven north of Georgetown's main drag. Comforting classics such as meatloaf, chicken pâté, and porridge are served up with an Asian spin. Desserts add a touch of exotica: The soy cheesecake elicits a Zen-like experience.

MAP 4 E3 **R17** 1039 33RD ST. NW
202-333-3888

CLYDE'S OF GEORGETOWN *AFTER HOURS • AMERICAN $$*
The local chain's original site opened here in 1963 and helped popularize upscale pub food. Revamped, the G-town location is always crowded with folks in for brews, burgers, and the signature chili (Elizabeth Taylor apparently used to have it shipped in). Try the new-in-2005 Chinatown location (707 7th St. NW, 202-349-3700) complete with takeout.

MAP 4 E4 **R27** 3236 M ST. NW
202-333-9180 WWW.CLYDES.COM

MICHEL RICHARD CITRONELLE *BUSINESS • FRENCH $$$*
Culinary genius Michel Richard, whose California-French creations are whimsical and unpredictable, presides over this Latham Hotel restaurant. Inspired by the marketplace, Richard invents new dishes each day. The menu offers two prix-fixe options only, but both are gastronomic treats.

MAP 4 E5 **R35** THE LATHAM HOTEL, 3000 M ST. NW
202-625-2150 WWW.CITRONELLEDC.COM

MORTON'S OF CHICAGO *BUSINESS • AMERICAN $$$*
One of several Morton's in the D.C. area, this dinner-only destination is set in historic Georgetown and surrounded by shops,

MICHEL RICHARD
CITRONELLE

PÂTISSERIE POUPON

attracting a bustling crowd of locals and tourists alike. The chain's
formula is simple: clubby surroundings, impeccable service, top-
grade beef, and mammoth meals.

MAP 4 E4 R19   3251 PROSPECT ST. NW
      202-342-6258   WWW.MORTONS.COM

PÂTISSERIE POUPON   *CAFÉ • FRENCH*   *$*

The incredible pastries, beautiful marzipan confections, and
creative salads at Pâtisserie Poupon are the extras; the real
reason to come here is for the best cup of French roast this side
of the Atlantic.

MAP 4 B3 R3   1645 WISCONSIN AVE. NW
      202-342-3248

PEACOCK CAFÉ   *CAFÉ*   *$$$*

A youthful crowd hangs out at this unpretentious yet chic café
for endless cups of coffee. Enjoy a libation with a selection from
the menu of salads, sandwiches, and vegetarian plates. Weekend
brunches are almost obligatory if you are in the neighborhood.

MAP 4 E4 R21   3251 PROSPECT ST. NW
      202-625-2740   WWW.PEACOCKCAFE.COM

SEASONS   *BUSINESS • AMERICAN*   *$$$*

Situated in a fashionable Georgetown hotel, this posh restaurant defines contemporary American sophistication. Lush
garden greenery complements such extravagant offerings as
lamb rack with braised shank and crab cakes. Breakfasts balance the healthful with the decadent – Bircher muesli versus
buttermilk pancakes – and lunches and dinners follow suit.

MAP 4 E6 R37   THE FOUR SEASONS HOTEL, 2800 PENNSYLVANIA AVE. NW
      202-342-0444   WWW.FOURSEASONS.COM

1789 RESTAURANT   *ROMANTIC • AMERICAN*   *$$$*

Set in a stately Federal-style townhouse, renowned 1789 takes
its name from the year that Georgetown was first incorporated
and retains an air of Old World gentility. The menu changes
daily, but keep an eye out for the thick pork chops and the
oyster bisque.

MAP 4 E2 R12   1226 36TH ST. NW
      202-965-1789   WWW.1789RESTAURANT.COM

MAP 5 | DUPONT CIRCLE

AL TIRAMISU *ROMANTIC • ITALIAN* $$$

This Dupont Circle hideaway serves up scrumptious Italian favorites – black truffles, imported branzino, and duck with balsamic vinegar and honey sauce, for example – in cozy booths that are perfect for a romantic tryst. Beware: the luscious specials are sure to induce sticker shock.

MAP 5 B4 ⓡ 25 2014 P ST. NW
202-467-4466 WWW.ALTIRAMISU.COM

BLUE DUCK TAVERN *BUSINESS • AMERICAN* $$$

At this Tony Chi–designed neighborhood grill, the kitchen isn't all that's out in the open. Farm-fresh produce and freshly caught seafood appears on the menu complete with region of origin and where it was harvested.

MAP 5 D3 ⓡ 45 1201 24TH ST. NW
202-419-6755 WWW.BLUEDUCKTAVERN.COM

DISH *HOT SPOTS • AMERICAN* $$$

Dish, at the homey River Inn, is a whimsical tribute to American cooking. Everything here, from the classic meatloaf to the brassy BLT, tastes like something Mom used to make, only better. In the winter, enjoy dinner by the roaring fireplace.

MAP 5 E2 ⓡ 60 THE RIVER INN, 924 25TH ST. NW
202-338-8707 WWW.THERIVERINN.COM

FAMOUS LUIGI'S *ROMANTIC • ITALIAN* $$

Red-checkered tablecloths, free-flowing wine, and a strolling flower salesman – Luigi's is straight out of *The Godfather*. Dine on hearty portions of garlicky red-sauce fare inside the dark, noisy dining room or on the roomier glass-encased porch. On busy weekend nights, takeout pizza and pasta is the way to go.

MAP 5 D5 ⓡ 50 1132 19TH ST. NW
202-331-7574 WWW.FAMOUSLUIGIS.COM

GALILEO *BUSINESS • ITALIAN* $$$

Always one of Washington's hottest reservations (and more popular than ever since Roberto Donna's appearances on *Iron Chef America*), Galileo draws politicos, power couples, and expense-account types with fine northern Italian cuisine and a formal dining atmosphere. The dinner-only osteria offers the same quality cuisine for bargain prices.

MAP 5 D4 ⓡ 48 1110 21ST ST. NW
202-293-7191 WWW.GALILEODC.COM

KAZ SUSHI BISTRO *BUSINESS • SUSHI* $$$

Renowned sushi chef Kaz Okochi tackles traditional sushi with a creative hand, often pairing the best of East and West. Beyond sushi, the menu presents several grilled specialties and artful bento boxes of tempura, rice, and meat. The cool, jade Asian decor sets a lovely scene.

MAP 5 E5 ⓡ 62 1915 I ST. NW
202-530-5500 WWW.KAZSUSHIBISTRO.COM

GALILEO KRAMERBOOKS & AFTERWORDS

KRAMERBOOKS & AFTERWORDS   *AFTER HOURS • AMERICAN* $$
This bookstore/café is better for browsing than grazing, but it's still a big draw for the black-turtleneck crowd. Discuss Kafka and capitalism with your waiter, or start that novel you always meant to write while lingering over a gigantic veggie omelet.

MAP 5 B5 ℝ28   1517 CONNECTICUT AVE. NW
202-387-1400   WWW.KRAMERS.COM

LUNA GRILL   *AMERICAN • BREAKFAST* $
It's eggs and pancakes anytime at this earthy Dupont Circle coffee shop. Vegetarians love the assortment of creative salads, and make-your-own pastas are always a big hit with the kids. In need of comfort food? The meatloaf and mashed potatoes always hits the spot.

MAP 5 C5 ℝ37   1301 CONNECTICUT AVE. NW
202-835-2280   WWW.LUNAGRILLANDDINER.COM

MARCEL'S   *ROMANTIC • FLEMISH* $$$
Chef/owner Robert Wiedmaier draws on his Belgian heritage while working culinary magic in Marcel's open kitchen. Enjoy the tasteful yet casual environs while sampling the seasonal menu studded with the likes of Coquilles St. Jacques, goat-cheese terrine, and crisped soft-shell crabs.

MAP 5 D2 ℝ44   2401 PENNSYLVANIA AVE. NW
202-296-1166   WWW.MARCELSDC.COM

MARK AND ORLANDO'S   *HOT SPOTS • AMERICAN* $$$
Downstairs, Mark serves cheeseburgers and crab cakes. Upstairs, Orlando handles upscale offerings such as mahimahi and venison. Thanks to the varied menu and chipper service, this split-level row house with a split personality is a hit among its diverse Dupont clientele of young and old, hipster and CEO.

MAP 5 B4 ℝ23   2020 P ST. NW
202-223-8463   WWW.MARKANDORLANDOS.COM

OBELISK   *ROMANTIC • ITALIAN* $$$
This is one of the city's finest purveyors of Italian countryside cooking. Delicious seasonal ingredients and a dedicated staff give the simple dining room a familial vibe. The five-course, prix-fixe menu lures repeat customers both young and old.

MAP 5 B4 ℝ21   2029 P ST. NW
202-872-1180

PIZZERIA PARADISO   21P

RESTAURANTS

PESCE   *HOT SPOTS • SEAFOOD $$$*

D.C.'s top chefs earned their toques at this small, noisy restaurant off Dupont Circle. Despite high turnover in the kitchen, this seafood standout turns out consistently high-quality fish dishes in a minimalist dining room filled with neighborhood scenesters and twentysomethings on dates.

MAP 5 B4 ® 24   2016 P ST. NW
202-466-3474

◖ PIZZERIA PARADISO   *QUICK BITES • PIZZA $$*

The line out the door at the Dupont branch is testimony to the unflagging popularity of the city's most famous pizzeria, which also offers tasty panini and salads. For a more leisurely evening out, visit the roomier Georgetown outpost (3282 M St. NW, 202-337-1245), its gustatory equal.

MAP 5 B4 ® 20   2029 P ST. NW
202-223-1245   WWW.EATYOURPIZZA.COM

POTBELLY SANDWICH WORKS   *QUICK BITES • SANDWICHES $*

When it comes to bang for your buck, it's tough to beat Potbelly. The counter service is friendly, the shakes are frosty, and the sandwiches – crusty baguettes loaded with fillings – always satisfy. All this plus live music comes for less than $5 a pop.

MAP 5 A5 ® 5   1635 CONNECTICUT AVE. NW
202-265-8890   WWW.POTBELLY.COM

PRIME RIB   *BUSINESS • AMERICAN $$$*

The jacket-and-tie requirement sets a standard where "anything goes" is the dress code nearly everywhere else. From the leopard skin rug and the leather booths to the tuxedoed waitstaff serving D.C.'s best beef, Prime Rib is unabashed indulgence.

MAP 5 E4 ® 61   2020 K ST. NW
202-466-8811   WWW.THEPRIMERIB.COM

RAKU   *QUICK BITES • PAN-ASIAN $*

Raku's tapas-style roster of both large and small plates travels across Asia for inspiration, enticing Gen X diners with excellent renditions of noodle soup, satays, wontons, and sushi. Although the service is often sluggish, the large specialty drinks and the superb see-and-be-seen outdoor patio more than make up for it.

MAP 5 A5 ® 13   1900 Q ST. NW
202-265-7258

SETTE OSTERIA   *HOT SPOT • PIZZA/ITALIAN $$*
Strollers and cell phones are popular accessories at this yuppie nouveau Italian osteria. While the pastas and pizzas are passable, they're hardly the main event: Sette's calming patio is the chicest place to sip a glass of wine and watch Dupont denizens strut by.

MAP **5** A4 **R 2**   1666 CONNECTICUT AVE. NW
202-483-3070   WWW.SETTEOSTERIA.COM

21P   *ROMANTIC • FUSION $$*
Comfy booths and comfort food make this a perfect pick-me-up. There aren't many surprises on the menu, but well-done classics like Cajun meatloaf and roast chicken keep regulars coming back for more. For a real bargain, pop in on Monday or Tuesday for half-priced wine.

MAP **5** B4 **R 22**   2100 P ST. NW
202-223-3824   WWW.21PRESTAURANT.COM

VIDALIA   *BUSINESS • SOUTHERN $$$*
Named after an onion that's a staple in Southern cooking, subterranean Vidalia lures diners with sunny walls, a sleek wine bar, and a menu of thoughtful twists on Southern favorites, like rabbit saddle and stuffed quail.

MAP **5** D5 **R 49**   1990 M ST. NW
202-659-1990   WWW.BISTROBIS.COM/VIDALIA

MAP 6 | 14TH AND U

ACADIANA   *BUSINESS • SOUTHERN $$$*
D.C. star chef Jeff Tunks takes guests down South with his dignified riff on po'boys, jambalaya, and étouffée. The space is more boardroom than Bourbon Street, but that hasn't stopped the crowds of politicos and conventioneers from lining up since it opened in 2005.

MAP **6** F5 **R 60**   901 NEW YORK AVE. NW
202-408-8848   WWW.ACADIANARESTAURANT.COM

AL CROSTINO   *HOT SPOTS • ITALIAN $$*
Slip out of the U Street madness and into this mellow addition to the strip, where you can sip wines by the glass while sampling house specialties such as the cured meats and cheeses. Best of all, it's all served without a whiff of attitude.

MAP **6** A4 **R 13**   1324 U ST. NW
202-797-0523   WWW.ALCROSTINO.COM

◖ BAR PILAR   *AFTER HOURS • FUSION $*
With an updated menu featuring flashier favorites like tuna tartare, Bar Pilar attracts sophisticated diners without forgetting its younger fan base: The kitchen still serves up comforting standards like lamb chops and the restaurant has kept its late-night hours.

MAP **6** B3 **R 21**   1833 14TH ST. NW
202-265-1751   WWW.BARPILAR.COM

RESTAURANTS

☾ BEN'S CHILI BOWL *AFTER HOURS • AMERICAN $*

Anchoring the edge of a once-shadowy stretch of U Street, this mom-and-pop institution has been slinging spicy chili, hot dogs, and other diner favorites for generations. Place your order at the counter and take a seat next to hungry locals, partying college students, and bewildered tourists.

MAP 6 A4 ℝ 16 1213 U ST. NW
202-667-0909 WWW.BENSCHILIBOWL.COM

BUSBOYS AND POETS *AFTER HOURS • AMERICAN $$*

Busboys and Poets is a restaurant, bookstore, and event space, all assembled into one hip locale. The chill vibe makes the already good food – wings, pizza, pork chops – taste even nicer. Come with a stroller or in hopes of finding a date – it's an equal-opportunity hangout.

MAP 6 A3 ℝ 7 2021 14TH ST. NW
202-387-7638 WWW.BUSBOYSANDPOETS.COM

CAFÉ LUNA *QUICK BITES • AMERICAN $*

Luna is a fun, no-frills spot for good, cheap pizza and pasta. The decor is limited to shards of mirror on one wall and chalkboard lists of specials on the other – quick food is definitely the focus here. Vegetarian and low-fat dishes abound.

MAP 6 C2 ℝ 31 1633 P ST. NW
202-387-4005

CAPITAL Q *QUICK BITES • BARBECUE $$*

This no-frills barbecue shack in the heart of Chinatown is a favorite of starving students and swank politicians alike. Paper plates, paper napkins, and the tangiest barbecue sauce this side of Texas that turns skeptics into regulars at the first bite.

MAP 6 F6 ℝ 64 707 H ST. NW
202-347-8396

CORDUROY *BUSINESS • AMERICAN $$$*

It may be concealed inside a Sheraton, but this serene hideaway is more than just a hotel restaurant. Guests who seek it out are rewarded with magical slow-braised pork belly and moist roast chicken in a cloistered setting ideal for secret rendezvous and solo dining alike.

MAP 6 F4 ℝ 57 FOUR POINTS SHERATON, 1201 K ST. NW
202-589-0699 WWW.FOURPOINTSWASHINGTONDC.COM

CRÈME CAFÉ *HOT SPOTS • SOUTHERN $$*

Known as the cream of the U Street crop, Crème carries home cooking to new heights. Chicken soup, shrimp and grits, and short ribs satisfy hungry locals clamoring for a seat in this spot no bigger than Mom's kitchen.

MAP 6 A4 ℝ 14 1322 U ST. NW
202-234-1884

ETETE *ROMANTIC • ETHIOPIAN $*

This stylish sanctuary a few blocks from the convention center is breathing new life into a quickly gentrifying area. Feast on *injera* (spongy Ethiopian bread) dolloped with a smattering of colorful meats and vegetables. These edible canvases are delicious, but they arrive slowly; prepare to linger.

`MAP 6` **A5 R 20**   1942 9TH ST. NW
202-232-7600   WWW.ETETERESTAURANT.COM

GEORGIA BROWN'S   *BUSINESS • SOUTHERN* $$$

This lively joint serves up the best of Southern Low Country cooking, where Hoppin' Jon rice and collard greens share the stage with surf 'n' turf. Dine under a tangle of metal kudzu that floats from the ceiling. Expect a boisterous crowd.

`MAP 6` **F3 R 56**   950 15TH ST. NW
202-393-4499   WWW.GBROWNS.COM

HANK'S OYSTER BAR   *HOT SPOTS • SEAFOOD* $$

An instant hit when it opened on a busy stretch of 17th Street, Hank's is part local hangout, part big night out. Chef Jamie Leeds serves up the classics, from fresh oysters (of course) to the tastiest lobster roll outside New England. On a warm summer night, the patio is the next best thing to the beach.

`MAP 6` **C2 R 27**   1624 Q ST. NW
202-462-4265   WWW.HANKSDC.COM

KOMI   *HOT SPOTS • NEW AMERICAN* $$$

Youthful Johnny Monis is D.C.'s hottest chef, and the crowds who pack his pencil-thin Komi know why. No-frills plates let seasonal produce sing – a refreshing concept on a strip of 17th Street that's hurting for gourmet options. The menu's always changing and the place is always packed; come early or learn to read lips.

`MAP 6` **C2 R 29**   1509 17TH ST. NW
202-332-9200   WWW.KOMIRESTAURANT.COM

LIMA   *HOT SPOTS • LATIN/WORLD* $$$

This trendy restaurant and nightclub is a budget-buster. For ceviche and *tiraditos*, descend into the sultry subterranean lounge. For fine dining, the posh upper level offers guinea hen and baked lobster at premium prices.

`MAP 6` **F3 R 54**   1401 K ST. NW
202-789-2800   WWW.LIMARESTAURANT.COM

LOVE CAFÉ   *CAFÉ* $

You'll feel like you wandered onto the set of *Friends* at this cozy café, an extension of the popular CakeLove bakery across the street. Students with laptops take up residence on the cushy couches; couples linger over coffee and delicious CakeLove pastries.

`MAP 6` **A3 R 6**   1501 U ST. NW
202-265-9800   WWW.CAKELOVE.COM

MATCHBOX   *QUICK BITES • PIZZA* $$

Now slightly bigger than its moniker after a 2006 expansion, this loud New York-style pizzeria doles out crisp pies, blistered to perfection in a hand-made 900-degree oven. If pizza isn't your thing, a full menu of American favorites awaits. You can't go wrong with tasty mini-burgers and a frosty beer.

`MAP 6` **F6 R 63**   713 H ST. NW
202-289-4441   WWW.MATCHBOXDC.COM

PIZZA

Washington may be the most powerful city in the world, but even power players had to start somewhere. It follows, then, that the city also swarms with students and interns, and that means one thing: plenty of cheap pizza. Thankfully, D.C. boasts many delicious spots for New York–style and Neapolitan pies that are cheap enough for bargain-seekers, yet chic enough to qualify as a night out. **Ella's Wood Fired Pizza (p. 24), Matchbox (p. 35),** and **2 Amys (p. 38)** have attracted loyal followers with their thin, crisp pies. Meanwhile, **Pizzeria Paradiso (p. 32),** a mainstay in Dupont Circle for years, has branched out to a Georgetown location. Roomier than the original, it's one of the rare Georgetown restaurants that is both cheap and delicious — and it even has a downstairs "birreria" for suds lovers.

MERKADO KITCHEN   *HOT SPOTS • FUSION $$*
An encyclopedic menu and coveted location make this eclectic choice sure to please even the wildest palate. Shrimp pad thai, wonton nachos, paella, and steaks compete for space on the diverse menu, while footloose singles compete for space at the buzzing bar.

MAP **6** C3 **R** 35   1443 P ST. NW   202-299-0018   WWW.MERKADODC.COM

RICE   *HOT SPOTS • THAI $$*
It's Thai with a twist at this noisy, high-energy restaurant (although it may look quiet and unassuming on the outside). The thoughtful menu reaches beyond the traditional with unusual items such as "spaghetti" spiked with Thai anchovies and bacon. Even the restaurant's namesake is special: All of the rice is flavored with coconut, instead of the traditionally steamed variety.

MAP **6** C3 **R** 32   1608 14TH ST. NW   202-234-2400

SUSHI TARO   *HOT SPOTS • SUSHI $$*
Sit at Washington's longest sushi bar and watch a small army of chefs slice and sculpt the freshest of fish. Or dine on mats at one of the low, traditional tables, where you can try the *kaiseki,* a formal 10-course menu highlighting the range of Japanese cuisine.

MAP **6** C2 **R** 30   1503 17TH ST. NW   202-462-8999   WWW.SUSHITARO.COM

VEGETATE   *HOT SPOTS • VEGETARIAN $$*
Vegetarians and the carnivores who love them come to this funky row house for inventive selections such as sesame-crusted tofu or veggie burgers with strawberry ketchup. Pea-colored walls give the impression of dining in a salad. The restaurant has struggled

to obtain a liquor license, but the Zen-like atmosphere and healthy menu may make boozing seem irrelevant.

MAP 6 D5 **R44**   1414 9TH ST. NW
202-232-4585   WWW.VEGETATEDC.COM

MAP 7 | UPPER NORTHWEST

ARDEO   *BUSINESS • NEW AMERICAN $$*
Cleveland Park's brashly hip New American hot spot serves up a seafood-heavy menu featuring jerk grilled mahimahi and blue-crab bisque, complemented by an opinionated, friendly staff. Small tables with stylish, wood-backed chairs fill the dining room, while mauve and sea-green booths line the walls.

MAP 7 B6 **R14**   3311 CONNECTICUT AVE. NW
202-244-6750   WWW.ARDEORESTAURANT.COM

CACTUS CANTINA   *HOT SPOTS • SOUTHWESTERN $$*
The sprawling expanse of Cactus Cantina is a testament to the popularity of Tex-Mex in D.C. Southwestern art, cowboy boots, and old photos of Mexican cowboys greet patrons at the entrance. Locals come back for the overflowing fajita platters and ample margaritas.

MAP 7 B2 **R11**   3300 WISCONSIN AVE. NW
202-686-7222   WWW.CACTUSCANTINA.COM

DINO   *ROMANTIC • ITALIAN $$*
This soothing *enoteca* brings a touch of Old World languidness to the bustling sidewalks of Cleveland Park. Snag a window seat, order a *cicchetti* and a glass of wine, and watch the world go by – without the phone. As the owners note on the menu, "Cell phones will be cooked on our Girrarosto!"

MAP 7 A6 **R4**   3435 CONNECTICUT AVE. NW
202-686-2966   WWW.DINO-DC.COM

INDIQUE   *HOT SPOTS • INDIAN $$*
Feast on a modern mix of Indian-style tapas and classics (think crisp samosas, dosas, and fiery vindaloos), graciously proffered in a dramatic two-level setting designed to resemble a personal residence. After a potent tamarind margarita – the restaurant's signature libation – you'll feel right at home.

MAP 7 A5 **R2**   3512-3514 CONNECTICUT AVE. NW
202-244-6600   WWW.INDIQUE.COM

LAVANDOU   *BUSINESS • FRENCH $$*
Lavandou doesn't wow crowds – it comforts them. The long-simmered *daube de boeuf* and roasted peppers stuffed with chèvre dissolve on the tongue. Relax and linger over the unpretentious flavors of Provence; the slow waitstaff gives you little alternative.

MAP 7 B6 **R12**   3321 CONNECTICUT AVE. NW
202-966-3002   WWW.LAVANDOURESTAURANT.NET

NAM VIET PHO – 79 *QUICK BITES • VIETNAMESE* $$

Forget about decor and service – just be glad for the effort that went into the menu. The selection of Vietnamese classics, from caramel pork to pho noodle soup, draws a steady crowd. One taste of the summer rolls dipped in peanut sauce and the barren walls are forgotten.

MAP 7 A6 R 5   3419 CONNECTICUT AVE. NW
202-237-1015

PALENA *HOT SPOTS • ITALIAN AND FRENCH* $$$

White House kitchen alumni Frank Ruta and Ann Amernick dish up some of D.C.'s finest Italian- and French-influenced fare. Luxuriate in the soft, romantic setting and be swept away by stellar service. Note to the budget conscious: Check out the nicely priced bar bargains.

MAP 7 A5 R 3   3529 CONNECTICUT AVE. NW
202-537-9250 WWW.PALENARESTAURANT.COM

SPICES ASIAN RESTAURANT
& SUSHI BAR *HOT SPOTS • PAN-ASIAN* $$

Pistachio- and smoke-hued walls, a blond-wood bar, and hand-made chopsticks contribute to the glossy chic of this uptown eatery. Sample raw fish, or indulge in bowls of silken udon noodles in crystalline broth. Gracious service blends with creative, contemporary Pan-Asian cuisine.

MAP 7 A6 R 8   3333-A CONNECTICUT AVE. NW
202-686-3833

TOWN HALL *HOT SPOTS • SOUTHERN* $$

Madras is in full effect at this Georgetown tavern, which gets the vote of neighborhood prepsters young and old (including, some say, the Bush twins). The food, from the shrimp scampi to the roasted chicken, is standard but satisfying, and the prices are more reasonable than other neighborhood haunts.

MAP 7 F3 R 20   2218 WISCONSIN AVE. NW
202-333-5641 WWW.TOWNHALLDC.COM

2 AMYS *QUICK BITES • PIZZA* $$

Authentic, crisp Neapolitan pizza makes this cheery pizza parlor a neighborhood favorite. Delectable deviled eggs, salt-cod fritters, Marsala custard, and a sinful cheese platter are gourmet touches that are comparable to any upscale restaurant.

MAP 7 B2 R 10   3715 MACOMB ST. NW
202-885-5700 WWW.2AMYSPIZZA.COM

MAP 8 ADAMS MORGAN/WOODLEY PARK

AMSTERDAM FALAFEL SHOP *QUICK BITES • FALAFEL* $

Adams Morgan hipsters know that after a night of barhopping, nothing beats a crisp falafel slathered with addictive garlic mayonnaise – and they won't let the sarcastic cashiers and spartan decor discourage them from their prize. A creative toppings bar with several varieties of hot sauce also helps extinguish hangovers.

MAP 8 D5 R 19   2425 18TH ST. NW
202-234-1969

BISTROT DU COIN   *ROMANTIC • FRENCH* $$

"Cigarettes, cigars, oui!" reads the menu at this fuss-free Parisian bistro. Enjoy cassoulet, steak *frites,* or chocolate mousse under the cathedral ceiling. Or sidle up to the zinc bar to sip a Lillet and brush up on your French with the expatriates.

MAP 8 **F4 R 37**   1738 CONNECTICUT AVE. NW
202-234-6969   WWW.BISTROTDUCOIN.COM

CASHION'S EAT PLACE   *HOT SPOTS • AMERICAN* $$$

With retro family photos dotting the wall, this upscale American restaurant matches its motif with old-style service. The daily-changing menu is a mélange of simply prepared food focusing on the D.C. region and its seasons – don't miss the Potatoes Anna. Masterful martinis await at the raised bar.

MAP 8 **C5 R 8**   1819 COLUMBIA RD. NW
202-797-1819   WWW.CASHIONSEATPLACE.COM

LITTLE FOUNTAIN CAFÉ   *ROMANTIC • AMERICAN* $$

The perfect romantic getaway is just steps from Adams Morgan's busy main drag. Almost hidden, this basement bistro with low ceilings, oak beams, and a tiny bar has a mysterious, seductive air. Peruse the changing menu of simple Continental cuisine, with treats like coriander-seared tuna and sour cherry crips, with someone special.

MAP 8 **D5 R 22**   2339 18TH ST. NW
202-462-8100   WWW.LITTLEFOUNTAINCAFE.COM

MESKEREM   *HOT SPOTS • ETHIOPIAN* $$

In the heart of D.C.'s Little Addis Ababa, Meskerem offers authentic Ethiopian fare to match its alluring furnishings. Scoop up spicy *doro wat* chicken with spongy *injera* bread, and sip honey wine as you relax on cushions or carved-wood chairs. Vegetarian options abound.

MAP 8 **D5 R 20**   2434 18TH ST. NW
202-462-4100   WWW.MESKEREMONLINE.COM

OPEN CITY   *AFTER HOURS • DINER* $$

This Woodley Park diner occupies a coveted corner of real estate near Rock Creek Park, the zoo, and Dupont Circle, so it pulls in the crowds. Fuel up before a long day of sightseeing, or bring a date and unwind with a late-night burger and beer. But expect noise, crowds, and sometimes-scattered service.

MAP 8 **C3 R 3**   2331 CALVERT ST. NW
202-332-2331   WWW.OPENCITYDC.COM

PASTA MIA   *HOT SPOTS • ITALIAN* $$

With perennial pasta favorites served in portions likely to provide patrons with tomorrow's lunch, this unassuming Italian eatery fills up nightly with students, families, and hipsters. You may have to wait for a seat at one of the checkered-tablecloth tables, but it's well worth it.

MAP 8 **C5 R 5**   1790 COLUMBIA RD. NW
202-328-9114

◖ PERRY'S   *HOT SPOTS • NEW AMERICAN* $$$

Formerly notable more for its rooftop party scene than its

TEAISM   TRYST COFFEEHOUSE BAR AND LOUNGE

cuisine, Perry's has reworked its menu to offer delicious twists on New American cooking. Sushi, once the only attraction, now competes with seasonal specials such as roasted ostrich and pumpkin soup. Of course, the view from the rooftop is still as enticing as ever.

MAP 8 C5 R 6   1811 COLUMBIA RD. NW
202-234-6218 WWW.PERRYSADAMSMORGAN.COM

TEAISM   *CAFÉ • PAN-ASIAN $*

The tiny upstairs seating area at Teaism's R Street location, with its low ceiling, simple wooden decor, and hanging screens, offers welcome seclusion from the bustle of Dupont Circle. The menu is a colorful mélange of light pan-Asian fare and more than 20 teas. Don't miss the plum soup or the yummy breakfasts.

MAP 8 F4 R 40   2009 R ST. NW
202-667-3827 WWW.TEAISM.COM

TRYST COFFEEHOUSE BAR
AND LOUNGE   *QUICK BITES • SANDWICHES $*

Freshly baked cookies and breakfast pastries give way in the evening to beers and bourbon shots. People-watch from a recliner or loveseat while munching on one of the playful sandwich selections (named after regulars).

MAP 8 C5 R 12   2459 18TH ST. NW
202-232-5500 WWW.TRYSTDC.COM

OVERVIEW MAP

◖ CITYZEN   *HOT SPOTS • AMERICAN $$$*

The name of this culinary oasis in the glam Mandarin Oriental Hotel is on the tip of every local foodie's tongue. Star chef Eric Ziebold tempts the tastebuds with cutting-edge New American cuisine and a massive wine list, while the Zen-like design – mixing earth, water, fire, metal, and wood – soothes the senses.

OVERVIEW MAP **E4**   MANDARIN ORIENTAL, 1330 MARYLAND AVE. SW
202-787-6868 WWW.MANDARINORIENTAL.COM

NIGHTLIFE

Hippest lounge: **EIGHTEENTH STREET LOUNGE,** p. 45

Best beer on tap: **THE REEF,** p. 50

Best spot to meet a U.S. senator: **TUNE INN,** p. 43

Best vodka martinis: **RUSSIA HOUSE,** p. 50

Most inviting hotel bar: **TABARD INN,** p. 45

Best place to impress your date: **MIE N YU,** p. 44

Best year-round roof deck: **TABAQ BISTRO,** p. 48

CAPITOL LOUNGE   BILLY MARTIN'S TAVERN

MAP 1 | WESTERN MALL/FOGGY BOTTOM

ROUND ROBIN BAR *BAR*
The term "lobbying" was invented in the Willard's lobby bar, a dark green, studylike room where you can imagine – or see – people waiting in the leather chairs to meet with representatives.

MAP 1 B6 N 30 WILLARD INTERCONTINENTAL,
1401 PENNSYLVANIA AVE. NW
202-637-7348

SKY TERRACE *BAR*
Get a rooftop view of the whole city from this relaxed outdoor bar in the Hotel Washington. Expect a long – but worthwhile – wait in nice weather. Open April-October only.

MAP 1 B6 N 28 HOTEL WASHINGTON, 515 15TH ST. NW
202-638-5900 WWW.HOTELWASHINGTON.COM

MAP 2 | SMITHSONIAN/PENN QUARTER

THE ELEPHANT AND CASTLE *BAR*
An expansive patio, robust beer list, and close proximity to the Mall draw a mix of soccer fans, British expats, and suits from local offices to this English-style pub chain. Beer lovers shouldn't miss the hand-pulled Fuller's Porter.

MAP 2 C2 N 28 1201 PENNSYLVANIA AVE. NW
202-347-7707 WWW.ELEPHANTCASTLE.COM

INDEBLEU *BAR*
The cocktail menu, designed to look like the D.C. subway map, catalogs 50-plus specialty drinks, including lychee-flavored martinis and blackberry mojitos. French-, Latin-, and Middle East-infused lounge music, occasional celeb sightings, and warm decor compensate for the high prices.

MAP 2 A4 N 5 707 G ST. NW
202-333-2538 WWW.BLEU.COM/INDEBLEU

POSTE *BAR*
Once the mail-sorting room of the 19th-century Old General Post Office, this architectural marvel of a restaurant/bar offers down-tempo electronica, herb-infused cocktails, and a warm-weather courtyard.

MAP 2 B4 N 23 THE HOTEL MONACO, 555 8TH ST. NW
202-783-6060 WWW.POSTEBRASSERIE.COM

MAP 3 CAPITOL HILL

BULLFEATHERS *BAR*
Named after one of Teddy Roosevelt's expletives, Bullfeathers caters to Capitol Hill staffers. You may even catch sight of your representative having drinks in this large early 1900s–style space.

MAP 3 F3 N 32 410 1ST ST. SE
202-543-5005

CAPITOL LOUNGE *PUB*
Recently renovated after a fire in early 2006, this pub remains a classic gathering place on the Hill, with brass fixtures, two well-kept pool tables, and political memorabilia. Congressmen, lobbyists, staffers, and a slightly younger crowd flock to it after a busy day on the Hill.

MAP 3 E4 N 23 229 PENNSYLVANIA AVE. SE
202-547-2098

POUR HOUSE *BAR*
Three unique floors – a German *biergarten* in the basement, a sports bar on the ground floor, and a plush lounge upstairs – make this the Hill's most eclectic nightspot and a destination worth crossing town for.

MAP 3 E4 N 25 319 PENNSYLVANIA AVE. SE
202-546-1001 WWW.POLITIKI-DC.COM

TUNE INN *PUB*
Established in 1947, D.C.'s best dive starts serving beer at 8 A.M. Cheap drinks and packed tables keep company with an eclectic mix of photos and hunting trophies on the walls.

MAP 3 E4 N 26 331 1/2 PENNSYLVANIA AVE. SE
202-543-2725

MAP 4 GEORGETOWN

BILLY MARTIN'S TAVERN *PUB*
Georgetown's oldest pub drips with history. Once a Civil War prison and Corcoran family art gallery, it has served hearty comfort food and drinks to every U.S. president since Harry Truman.

MAP 4 E4 N 22 1264 WISCONSIN AVE. NW
202-333-7370 WWW.MARTINS-TAVERN.COM

MIE N YU   BLUE GIN

BLUE GIN   *LOUNGE/DANCE CLUB*

Cleverly tucked away from the bustle of Wisconsin Avenue, Blue Gin boasts a strong roster of DJs and a chic ambience that set it apart from Georgetown's pub-centric nightlife scene.

MAP 4   E4 **Ⓝ23**   1206 WISCONSIN AVE. NW
202-965-5555   WWW.BLUEGINDC.COM

BLUES ALLEY   *MUSIC CLUB*

A local landmark since 1965, this intimate supper club has hosted some of the greatest names in jazz, such as Dizzy Gillespie and Sarah Vaughan. Enjoy spicy Creole cuisine with the music.

MAP 4   F4 **Ⓝ39**   1073 WISCONSIN AVE. NW
202-337-4141   WWW.BLUESALLEY.COM

THE GARDEN TERRACE LOUNGE   *LOUNGE*

An oasis of calm just outside the Georgetown mayhem, this scenic spot draws distinguished guests such as celebrities, performers from the Kennedy Center, and foreign dignitaries. Expansive windows overlook the C&O Canal and the large outdoor terrace.

MAP 4   E6 **Ⓝ37**   FOUR SEASONS HOTEL, 2800 PENNSYLVANIA AVE. NW
202-342-0444
WWW.FOURSEASONS.COM/WASHINGTON/LOUNGE_5.HTML

◖ MIE N YU   *BAR*

Striking Asian decor – elegant hanging lanterns, gold statues of Hindu gods – sets the scene at this chic restaurant/bar. The outstanding wine selection will make you want to sample all night long.

MAP 4   E5 **Ⓝ29**   3125 M ST. NW
202-333-6122   WWW.MIENYU.COM

SEQUOIA   *BAR*

Business casual mixes with boat-bum attire at Sequoia's multilevel patio on the Potomac – *the* place to see and be seen on a sunny day. The waterfront views also make it a good, if pricey, place to bring a date.

MAP 4   F5 **Ⓝ43**   3000 K ST. NW
202-944-4200

MAP 5 DUPONT CIRCLE

BRICKSKELLER *BAR*
Interesting beer bottles decorate the small, basement-level brick rooms of this beer-lover's heaven. The wood tables and barren decor may not impress, but the global assortment of 500 brews certainly will.

MAP 5 B3 Ⓝ14   1523 22ND ST. NW
202-293-1885 WWW.THEBRICKSKELLER.COM

CAFE CITRON *DANCE CLUB*
When the weather is warm, the weekend starts early at this three-story dance club popular with the young professional and international sets. Expect large crowds reveling to salsa and merengue Wednesday–Saturday nights.

MAP 5 C5 Ⓝ36   1343 CONNECTICUT AVE. NW
202-530-8844

◖ EIGHTEENTH STREET LOUNGE *LOUNGE*
An unmarked door leads into this multistory lounge and dance club. Run by the group that owns the Eighteenth Street Lounge music label, this is the best place in town to hear hip new lounge, world, and electronica sounds.

MAP 5 C5 Ⓝ41   1212 18TH ST. NW
202-466-3922

FIVE *DANCE CLUB*
In D.C.'s floundering nightclub scene, Five is a guiding light, featuring superstar DJs and hip-hop events, a multilevel club environment (including a Caribbean-theme roof deck), modest cover fees, and no dress code.

MAP 5 C5 Ⓝ38   1214-B 18TH ST. NW
202-331-7123 WWW.FIVEDC.COM

OZIO *LOUNGE*
This high-end martini and cigar bar is located in a neighborhood that otherwise caters to a younger crowd. Dress up and pay a cover on weekends to get into the dimly lit, ochre-colored digs.

MAP 5 C5 Ⓝ40   1813 M ST. NW
202-822-6000 WWW.OZIODC.COM

◖ TABARD INN *BAR*
Gaze into a fireplace while sipping after-dinner drinks on a couch in one of a series of intimate rooms scattered throughout this bed-and-breakfast inn; you'll feel like you're a guest in a friend's beautiful townhouse.

MAP 5 C6 Ⓝ42   1739 N ST. NW
202-331-8528 WWW.TABARDINN.COM

BLACK CAT   AROMA

NIGHTLIFE

TOWN & COUNTRY LOUNGE *LOUNGE*

A sparse, well-dressed crowd frequents this piano lounge in the fashionable Mayflower Hotel. The elegant decor includes a marble bar, leather chairs, and wooden furnishings.

MAP **5** D6 Ⓝ54 RENAISSANCE MAYFLOWER HOTEL,
1127 CONNECTICUT AVE. NW
202-347-3000

MAP 6 | 14TH AND U

BLACK CAT *MUSIC CLUB*

This rock-and-roll haven opens its doors seven nights a week for large crowds who come to enjoy the diverse range of buzz-worthy alternative bands and DJ events. A no-cover side bar also makes for a great local's dive.

MAP **6** B3 Ⓝ24 1811 14TH ST. NW
202-667-7960 (BAR); 202-667-7960 (CONCERT LINE)
WWW.BLACKCATDC.COM

BOHEMIAN CAVERNS *JAZZ CLUB*

You can get supper, but music is the reason people flock to Washington's oldest jazz club. Upstairs is a proper restaurant, while the cavernous downstairs embodies its name, complete with faux stalactites.

MAP **6** A5 Ⓝ18 2001 11TH ST. NW
202-299-0801 WWW.BOHEMIANCAVERNS.COM

CAFE NEMA *JAZZ CLUB*

This Somali-owned hot spot recently graduated from a tiny base-ment bar to a three-story club with a growing roster of established jazz musicians, hip-hop events, and DJs – all sans cover charge.

MAP **6** A4 Ⓝ12 1334 U ST. NW
202-667-3215 WWW.CAFENEMA.COM

CAFÉ SAINT-EX/GATE 54 *BAR*

Upstairs, Saint-Ex features a polished wooden bar, a small warm-weather patio, aviation decor, and a fine menu of classic and

U STREET MUSIC

Jazz has thrived along U Street ever since the days when Duke Ellington lived here in the early 1900s. Today, **Bohemian Caverns (p. 46)** is the largest and best-known jazz venue, but for more intimate sessions check out Twins Jazz (1344 U St. NW, 202-234-0072), **Cafe Nema (p. 46),** and **HR-57 (p. 79)**. This neighborhood also boasts D.C.'s best rock music scene. With two excellent stages, the **Black Cat (p. 46)** is the best place in town to catch rising stars. Virtually every big alternative act in recent memory, from Radiohead to the White Stripes, rocked this house before going mainstream. The **9:30 Club (p. 47),** one block north of U Street, is a bona fide East Coast musical institution. Locals also love the **Velvet Lounge** (915 U St. NW, 202-462-3213) and **DC9** (1940 9th St. NW, 202-483-5000), two smaller clubs regularly buzzing with great talent.

contemporary European cuisine. Downstairs is Gate 54, a friendly hipster lounge where DJs spin different genres each night.

MAP 6 A3 11 1847 14TH ST. NW
202-265-7839 WWW.SAINT-EX.COM

CHI-CHA LOUNGE *LOUNGE*
Comfy velvet couches and Peruvian appetizers are the signatures of this dimly lit lounge. The semi-regular live jazz often fills the place up, but it's still intimate enough for conversation.

MAP 6 A2 2 1624 U ST. NW
202-234-8400

HALO *QUEER*
A clear circle embossed on frosted glass marks the facade of this stylish Logan Circle lounge. It may be tiny, but sleek leather furniture, chill lighting, and seating for 80 percent of its patrons dispel any sense of overcrowding.

MAP 6 C3 36 1435 P ST. NW
202-797-9730 WWW.HALODC.COM

LOCAL 16 *BAR*
Affordable cocktails and cozy red walls with black-and-white photos of D.C.'s punk heyday make Local 16 a refreshing alternative to swankier spots. Heaters on the expansive wooden deck upstairs make the outdoors accessible in almost all seasons.

MAP 6 A2 3 1602 U ST. NW
202-265-2828

9:30 CLUB *MUSIC CLUB*
This icon of punk accommodates 1,000 dancing, drinking guests and now hosts a wider range of talent, including the likes of The

Roots, Dolly Parton, and Sonic Youth. Escape to the downstairs bar to avoid the crush.

MAP 6 A5 N 19   815 V ST. NW
202-265-0930 (CONCERT LINE)   WWW.930.COM

TABAQ BISTRO   *BAR*

Year-round views of the Capitol dome and the Washington Monument can be had from the expansive fourth-floor roof deck of this multi-level lounge; retractable glass keeps it seasonally appropriate. Candlelight, small plates, cocktails, and an amenable staff round out the experience.

MAP 6 A3 N 10   1336 U ST. NW
202-265-0965   WWW.TABAQDC.COM

U-TOPIA   *BAR*

Looking like a below-ground Paris jazz cave, U-topia was among the first on U Street's hot nightlife scene, and it's still going strong. Great food tags along with the live jazz and blues.

MAP 6 A3 N 9   1418 U ST. NW
202-483-7669   WWW.UTOPIAINDC.COM

MAP 7   UPPER NORTHWEST

AROMA   *BAR*

The creative bartenders at this swank martini bar mix clever drink variations, such as a metropolitan with fresh raspberries. Brightly colored modernistic furnishings make the back lounge a stylish place to relax with a group.

MAP 7 A6 N 6   3417 CONNECTICUT AVE. NW
202-244-7995

BARDEO   *WINE BAR*

A wine bar with shiny, modern decor and frequented by a heady mix of twenty- and thirtysomething professionals, Bardeo offers numerous tables for intimate tête-à-têtes and a wide range of reasonably priced wines.

MAP 7 B6 N 15   3311 CONNECTICUT AVE. NW
202-244-6550   WWW.BARDEO.COM

MAP 8   ADAMS MORGAN/WOODLEY PARK

BEDROCK BILLIARDS   *POOL HALL*

This friendly, basement-level pool hall is a locals' joint, with darts, a wide variety of beer and wine, top-shelf liquor, and pay-by-the-hour tables. The decor is thrift-store kitsch, with 1950s furniture and local art adorning the walls.

MAP 8 D5 N 17   1841 COLUMBIA RD. NW
202-667-7665   WWW.BEDROCKBILLIARDS.COM

NIGHTLIFE

MADAM'S ORGAN   BOURBON

BOURBON *BAR*

More than 50 varieties of the bar's namesake are on offer, but even non-bourbon-lovers will enjoy the pub's three levels of café-style seating, back patio, easy-going staff, and eclectic indie-rock soundtrack.

MAP 8 D5 23 2321 18TH ST. NW
202-332-0800

FELIX/SPY LOUNGE *LOUNGE*

Two identities comprise this double agent of nightspots. N.Y.C.-infused Felix serves up live jazz and funk with great food (try the crab cakes) and superb specialty drinks such as the lychee-infused Lotus martini; Spy Lounge has an L.A.-esque ultrachic decor and a DJ-spun soundtrack.

MAP 8 D5 ❶21 2406 18T H ST. NW
202-483-3549   WWW.THEFELIX.COM

HABANA VILLAGE BAR AND RESTAURANT *BAR*

Wildly popular salsa and tango lessons bring this bar to life Wednesday–Saturday. Dark wooden walls and gorgeous Latin American hunting masks make for a classy decor, and the sweet, bubbly mojitos are unforgettable.

MAP 8 C5 ❶9 1834 COLUMBIA RD. NW
202-462-6310

MADAM'S ORGAN *MUSIC CLUB*

Redheads get half-priced Rolling Rocks at this live-music venue specializing in rock, bluegrass, Latin music, and good Southern cooking. The motto says it all: "Where the beautiful people go to get ugly."

MAP 8 C5 ❶11 2461 18TH ST. NW
202-667-5370   WWW.MADAMSORGAN.COM

PHARAOH'S ROCK-N-BLUES BAR AND GRILL *MUSIC CLUB*

The decor – an unusual mix of rock iconography and Egyptian artifacts – characterizes the eclectic nature of this live-music venue, where there's no cover, no pretension, inexpensive drinks, and a convivial atmosphere.

MAP 8 C5 ❶7 1817 COLUMBIA RD. NW
202-232-6009

◖ THE REEF *BAR*

Shimmering tropical fish tanks, a rainforest-themed street-level room, and a huge rooftop patio provide loads of eye candy at this hot nightspot. The all-draft beer selection is one of Adams Morgan's finest.

MAP 8 C5 ◑13   2446 18TH ST. NW
202-518-3800   WWW.THEREEFDC.COM

◖ RUSSIA HOUSE *LOUNGE*

Deep red damask-covered walls evoke a sense of Old-World comfort in a lounge that feels like a luxurious living room filled with well-dressed expats and urban hipsters. More than 50 types of vodkas are on offer, including several made in-house and infused with fresh fruit.

MAP 8 F4 ◑35   1800 CONNECTICUT AVE. NW
202-234-9433   WWW.RUSSIAHOUSELOUNGE.COM

NIGHTLIFE

S SHOPS

Best hangout for gastronomes: **COWGIRL CREAMERY,** p. 53

Best place to spend a Sunday: **EASTERN MARKET,** p. 54

Best place to buy a postcard: **PULP ON THE HILL,** p. 54

Hottest spot for the hottest sauces:
UNCLE BRUTHA'S HOT SAUCE EMPORIUM, p. 55

Most blissful beauty indulgence: **AVEDA,** p. 55

Most original souvenirs: **CHOCOLATE MOOSE,** p. 58

Quirkiest kitchenware: **GINZA,** p. 64

Best place to find a rare book:
SECOND STORY BOOKS & ANTIQUES, p. 60

Grooviest home decor: **TABLETOP,** p. 60

Best district for vintage shopping: **U STREET,** p. 62

MAP 1 WESTERN MALL/FOGGY BOTTOM

ALEX *CLOTHING*
The creations of fringe designers stock the shelves at this fun, family-owned, unisex boutique. The proprietors are huge champions of local talent, and the store's unusual Foggy Bottom location makes it a find among a maze of office buildings.

MAP 1 A4 ☻ 7 1919 PENNSYLVANIA AVE. NW
202-296-2610 WWW.ALEXBOUTIQUEDC.COM

AMERICAN INSTITUTE OF ARCHITECTS BOOKSTORE *BOOKS*
Located inside the A.I.A., this sleek store sells the latest books and periodicals on architecture and design, as well as unusual gifts with an architectural focus.

MAP 1 B5 ☻ 25 1735 NEW YORK AVE. NW
202-626-7541 WWW.AIA.ORG

TOWER RECORDS *MUSIC*
Tower was one of the first music megastores to arrive in D.C. and today draws browsers with two floors of music and video products.

MAP 1 A3 ☻ 3 2100 PENNSYLVANIA AVE. NW
202-331-2400 (MUSIC) OR 202-223-3900 (VIDEO)
WWW.TOWERRECORDS.COM

WORLD BANK INFOSHOP *BOOKS*
A playground for policy wonks, this large bookstore in the World Bank carries not best-selling fiction, but a very specialized collection focusing on the development and economy of various nations.

MAP 1 A4 ☻ 8 1818 H ST. NW
202-473-1000 WWW.WORLDBANK.ORG

MAP 2 SMITHSONIAN/PENN QUARTER

APARTMENT ZERO *GIFT AND HOME*
Step into this sleek store to find everything for the modern urban apartment: retro lamps, metallic picture frames and office accessories, as well as stylish wooden furniture.

MAP 2 C4 ☻ 35 406 7TH ST. NW
202-628-4067 WWW.APARTMENTZERO.COM

CELADON SPA *BATH, BEAUTY, AND SPA*
A pristine haven in a downtown dead zone, Celadon is a serene respite for tired nine-to-fivers and visitors who crave pampering; it offers everything from dreamlike pedicures to soothing wraps and massages.

MAP 2 B2 ☻ 10 1180 F ST. NW
202-347-3333 WWW.CELADONSPA.COM

CHAPTERS: A LITERARY BOOKSTORE *BOOKS*
A sizable independent bookstore, Chapters has a knowledgeable

CELADON SPA   COWGIRL CREAMERY

SHOPS

staff, a great collection of fiction, and a schedule of readings with renowned authors.

MAP 2 B3 **S17**   445 11TH ST. NW
202-737-5553

COWGIRL CREAMERY   *GOURMET GOODIES*
This California outpost showcases the company's award-winning cheeses, as well as wares from other small producers. The *fromage* fantasyland also offers breads, charcuterie, and wines, plus a tasting bar.

MAP 2 B4 **S18**   919 F ST. NW
202-393-6880   WWW.COWGIRLCREAMERY.COM

OLSSON'S BOOKS AND RECORDS   *BOOKS AND MUSIC*
One in D.C.'s oldest chain of independent book and music stores, the Penn Quarter branch leans toward books on policy and analysis issues. There's also a large arts and ancient history selection.

MAP 2 C4 **S33**   418 7TH ST. NW
202-638-7610   WWW.OLSSONS.COM

SOUVENIR STANDS   *GIFT AND HOME*
Get all your inexpensive souvenirs in one swift shot at the numerous vans that litter the Mall. The standing deal for years has been three D.C. T-shirts for about $10.

MAP 2 E2 **S47**   VARIOUS LOCATIONS ON THE MALL

MAP 3   CAPITOL HILL

ART & SOUL   *GIFT AND HOME*
Selling contemporary wearable art, jewelry, and crafts, this sophisticated little shop is the ideal place to find the perfect gift.

MAP 3 E4 **S22**   225 PENNSYLVANIA AVE. SE
202-548-0105

CLOTHES ENCOUNTERS OF A SECOND KIND   *CLOTHING*
This upscale consignment shop features only in-style and in-season

EASTERN MARKET PULP ON THE HILL

clothing. They carry hand-selected classic clothes and designer-name business suits at reasonable – though not cheap – prices.

MAP 3 E6 **S** 28 202 7TH ST. SE
202-546-4004

◖ EASTERN MARKET *SHOPPING DISTRICT*
This bustling indoor/outdoor bazaar attracts vendors from across the country selling exotic jewelry, rare records, and beautiful handmade furniture every weekend. Fresh seafood and gourmet treats are available daily.

MAP 3 E6 **S** 31 225 7TH ST. SE
202-544-0083 WWW.EASTERNMARKET.NET

FAIRY GODMOTHER *KIDS STUFF*
Carrying equal amounts of fiction and nonfiction, Fairy Godmother lines its shelves with children's and young adult books hand selected by the owner. Cool baby and creative arts toys give shoppers non-book options, too.

MAP 3 F6 **S** 35 319 7TH ST. SE
202-547-5474

FLIGHTS OF FANCY *KIDS STUFF*
Plush animals and marionettes comprise the decor, as well as the merchandise, of this well-stocked store. Also find an extensive collection of board games for both children and grown-ups.

MAP 3 B3 **S** 5 UNION STATION, 50 MASSACHUSETTS AVE. NE
202-371-9800

THE FORECAST *CLOTHING*
Helpful sales people will dress you up in luxurious, comfortable fabrics – silk, leather, suede, and velvet – from designers such as Eileen Fisher, Yansi Fugel, and Michael Stars.

MAP 3 E6 **S** 30 218 7TH ST. SE
202-547-7337

◖ PULP ON THE HILL *GIFT AND HOME*
This stationery store makes a statement with its unique writing materials, mod cards, and other hipster accoutrements that lure an edgy crowd to this Cap Hill location and its U Street outpost (1803 14th St. NW, 202-462-7857).

MAP 3 E4 **S** 24 303 PENNSYLVANIA AVE. SE
202-543-1924 WWW.PULPDC.COM

TROVER SHOP *BOOKS*
A local bookstore that's been in D.C. since the 1960s, Trover carries best sellers and a vast array of D.C. guidebooks and maps. Kid's books and greeting cards let you shop for others, too.

MAP 3 E4 S 20 221 PENNSYLVANIA AVE. SE
202-547-2665

◖ UNCLE BRUTHA'S
HOT SAUCE EMPORIUM *GOURMET GOODIES*
Culinary pyromaniacs flock to Uncle Brutha's for the massive selection (300 and counting) of fiery sauces — some homegrown, others from as far away as South Africa and Belize. The hot sauce-tasting bar allows you to try before you buy.

MAP 3 F6 S 34 323 7TH ST. SE
202-546-3473 WWW.UNCLEBRUTHA.COM

THE VILLAGE *CLOTHING*
An eclectic store with handcrafted items from around the world, the Village carries casual, comfortable clothing from Putumayo and Flax, in addition to various works of art and craft.

MAP 3 E6 S 27 705 NORTH CAROLINA AVE. SE
202-546-3040 WWW.THEVILLAGEONCAPITOLHILL.COM

WOVEN HISTORY/SILK ROAD *GIFT AND HOME*
One side of the store has woven rugs and tapestries from 30 locations in Asia, including Turkey and Nepal; the other side carries antique furniture, textiles, and art from countries along the Silk Road.

MAP 3 F6 S 33 311–315 7TH ST. SE
202-543-1705 WWW.WOVENHISTORY.COM

SHOPS

MAP 4 GEORGETOWN

A MANO *GIFT AND HOME*
A sliver of Europe at the top of the hill in Georgetown, this is the best place to find handmade French and Italian linens, ceramics, glass, and pottery. The uncommon old-world craftsmanship and solicitous service adds to the allure.

MAP 4 B3 S 2 1677 WISCONSIN AVE. NW
202-298-7200

◖ AVEDA *BATH, BEAUTY, AND SPA*
The Georgetown flagship store along with several outposts throughout the city are renowned for an all-natural approach to beauty: Products and treatments are derived from flowers and plants, and the shops also offer nutrition and wellness seminars.

MAP 4 D4 S 10 1325 WISCONSIN AVE. NW
202-965-1325 WWW.AVEDA.COM

BARNES & NOBLE BOOKSELLERS *BOOKS AND MUSIC*
Browse the books, sample some CDs, or sip an espresso at this

bustling three-level store. Look out for special events like book signings and readings by notable authors such as Scott Turow.

MAP 4   E5 **S 33**   3040 M ST. NW
202-965-9880   WWW.BARNESANDNOBLE.COM

BARNEY'S CO-OP   *CLOTHING*
Local fashionistas couldn't be happier that Washington finally has its very own Barney's. The Co-op fits right in among its Georgetown neighbors, offering only the hottest designers at Manhattan prices.

MAP 4   E5 **S 34**   3040 M ST. NW
202-350-5832   WWW.BARNEYSCOOP.COM

BOCONCEPT   *GIFT AND HOME*
This Danish furniture store offers sleek seating, lamps, accessories, and even stereo systems. The futuristic styles and minimalist colors (primarily black and white) appeal to modern sophisticates.

MAP 4   E3 **S 16**   3342 M ST. NW
202-333-5656   WWW.BOCONCEPT.COM

DEAN & DELUCA   *GOURMET GOODIES*
The gourmet store to end all gourmet stores, Dean & DeLuca has not only superb groceries, but also beautiful knives, pans, and even sushi mats in the back.

MAP 4   E4 **S 25**   3276 M ST. NW
202-342-2500   WWW.DEANANDDELUCA.COM

FIRE AND ICE   *JEWELRY*
Silver and semiprecious stones are the attention-grabbers, but glassware, numerous animal trinkets, and polished fossils are also on display at this special jewelry store.

MAP 4   E4 **S 27**   SHOPS AT GEORGETOWN PARK, 3222 M ST. NW
202-338-0024

HU'S SHOES   URBAN CHIC

GEORGETOWN   *SHOPPING DISTRICT*
Stomping ground of the impossibly thin, impossibly tan, and impossibly rich, Georgetown combines capitalism with historic charm. Upscale boutiques are situated near quaint row houses with cobblestone walkways, and mom-and-pop shops hold their own alongside mammoth chains.

MAP 4   E4 **$24**   M ST. BTWN. 27TH AND 35TH STS. NW; WISCONSIN AVE. BTWN. M AND S STS. NW

HU'S SHOES   *SHOES*
Make tracks to trendy Hu's for Marc Jacobs, Chloe, and Miss Trish, as well as up-and-coming names. The clientele tends to be older and more discriminating, and the prices are as steep as the stilettos.

MAP 4   E5 **$31**   3005 M ST. NW
202-342-0202   WWW.HUSHOES.COM

ROCHE SALON   *BATH, BEAUTY, AND SPA*
Considered one of the best cut-and-color shops in the city, this trendy salon is worth a visit just to see the wild and whimsical decor. The high-end hair and beauty products on sale include Kerastase from France, as well as their own Roche line.

MAP 4   F5 **$42**   3050 K ST. NW
202-775-0775   WWW.ROCHESALON.COM

SHOPS AT GEORGETOWN PARK   *SHOPPING DISTRICT*
Home to popular standbys such as Ann Taylor and J. Crew, as well as newer chains like H&M and Intermix, the Shops anchor several prime blocks of Georgetown real estate, making the neighborhood's unofficial pastime – spending money – almost too easy.

MAP 4   E4 **$28**   3222 M ST. NW
202-342-8190   WWW.SHOPSATGEORGETOWNPARK.COM

URBAN CHIC   *CLOTHING*
This Georgetown jewel offers as many designers as a major chain, yet retains the intimacy of a boutique. The well-heeled clientele loves the fawning attention, huge selection (more than 100 designers), and the superb denim collection.

MAP 4   C3 **$7**   1626 WISCONSIN AVE. NW
202-338-5398   WWW.URBANCHIC-DC.COM

MAP 5 DUPONT CIRCLE

BEADAZZLED *GIFT AND HOME*

Beadazzled has hundreds of containers, organized by color and filled with beads of every shape and size, from whimsical animals to semiprecious stones.

MAP 5 B5 **S** 29   1507 CONNECTICUT AVE. NW
202-265-2323   WWW.BEADAZZLED.NET

BLUE MERCURY *BATH, BEAUTY, AND SPA*

Carrying the most select (and expensive) facial products and make-up, Blue Mercury is a small chain that stocks magazine-referenced brands such as Bliss, Creed, and Trish McEvoy.

MAP 5 A5 **S** 12   1619 CONNECTICUT AVE. NW
202-462-1300   WWW.BLUEMERCURY.COM

BORDERS BOOKS AND MUSIC *BOOKS AND MUSIC*

In addition to the extensive book and music offerings, the full-scale cultural mix at Borders includes live jazz, wine tastings, film screenings, poetry slams, and author readings.

MAP 5 D5 **S** 52   1800 L ST. NW
202-466-4999   WWW.BORDERSTORES.COM

CHOCOLATE MOOSE *GIFT AND HOME*

This is a classy tchotchke store with amusing pins, hair accessories, candy, "bad girl" drink coasters, gag gifts, stickers, greeting cards, and games.

MAP 5 D6 **S** 55   1743 L ST. NW
202-463-0992   WWW.CHOCOLATEMOOSEDC.COM

CHURCH'S ENGLISH SHOES *SHOES*

At this old-school men's shoe store, someone will sit at your feet and measure your foot size before offering you a choice from the selection of classic, conservative leather shoes. Stop in here for the right shoes to wear to a meeting on the Hill.

MAP 5 D5 **S** 51   1820 L ST. NW
202-296-3366

CLAUDE TAYLOR PHOTOGRAPHY *KIDS STUFF*

The merchandise theme here is characters from French children's books: Babar lunchboxes, Tintin books, Little Prince mugs. There's also a great collection of Parisian photos and posters.

MAP 5 A5 **S** 6   1627 CONNECTICUT AVE. NW
202-518-4000

CUSTOM SHOP CLOTHIERS *CLOTHING*

At this men's clothier, you can get measured, choose the fabric, and in 6-8 weeks, get a shirt or suit that's tailored just for you. Styles are conservative, and prices range from $89 shirts to $1,000 suits.

MAP 5 D6 **S** 58   1033 CONNECTICUT AVE. NW
202-659-8250

CHOCOLATE MOOSE

KRAMERBOOKS & AFTERWORDS

DUPONT CIRCLE *SHOPPING DISTRICT*
Vibrant all day and into the night – many businesses stay open until 1 A.M. – Dupont is Washington's pulse. The mix of chic boutiques, independent bookstores, and see-and-be-seen eateries, all of which are gay friendly, ensure that you'll be well outfitted, well read, and well fed.

MAP 5 B5 **S 31**   CONNECTICUT AVE. BTWN. K AND S STS. NW

FRANZ BADER BOOKSTORE *BOOKS*
From coffee-table books to instructional manuals, art and art history are the focus here, in honor of the store's namesake. Find books on graphic arts, fine arts, photography, and architecture.

MAP 5 E5 **S 63**   1911 I ST. NW
202-337-5440

J & R CIGAR *GIFT AND HOME*
The floor-to-ceiling array of cigars comes from numerous countries – some as far-flung as Cameroon and Tanzania. Find handsome wooden humidors and other cigar paraphernalia, as well.

MAP 5 D6 **S 57**   1730 L ST. NW
202-296-3872

KRAMERBOOKS & AFTERWORDS *BOOKS*
This thriving independent bookstore shelves an excellent collection of new and local titles, along with impressive cookbook and travel sections. The café in the back provides a cozy spot to read.

MAP 5 B5 **S 28**   1517 CONNECTICUT AVE. NW
202-387-1400   WWW.KRAMERS.COM

LAMBDA RISING *BOOKS AND MUSIC*
The cheerful heart of Dupont's gay community, Lambda Rising was D.C.'s first bookstore for queer men and women when it was founded in 1974.

MAP 5 A5 **S 7**   1625 CONNECTICUT AVE. NW
202-462-6969   WWW.LAMBDARISING.COM

MELODY RECORDS *MUSIC*
The crammed aisles of popular music and rare finds at this no-frills storefront keep Dupont-area hipsters happy – even if the brooding folks behind the counter aren't.

MAP 5 A5 **S 8**   1623 CONNECTICUT AVE. NW
202-232-4002   WWW.MELODYRECORDS.COM

FLEA AND FARMERS MARKETS

Eastern Market (p. 54) is Washington's classic outdoor exchange – a year-round spectacle of antiques, furniture, jewelry, and exotic foods. But come the weekend, especially when the weather's warm, many D.C. neighborhoods play host to open-air farmers markets and flea markets, which are excellent sources of fresh produce, unique crafts, and other rare finds. **Dupont Circle (p. 59), Georgetown (p. 57),** and **Adams Morgan (on 18th St., p. 63)** offer weekend bazaars. Other neighborhoods host markets during the week: The Penn Quarter is home to a Thursday-evening version, and Foggy Bottom dwellers know that Wednesday is fresh produce night. These markets are a terrific way to meet residents and get great finds on the cheap: You'll see old ladies, families with kids, students, visitors, and sometimes even local bigwigs grazing the goods.

PROPER TOPPER *ACCESSORIES*
Originally just a hat store, Proper Topper now goes beyond fedoras and glamorous cloches; scarves, gloves, jewelry, and wonderful bath soaps add even more elegance.

MAP 5 C5 ⑨35 1350 CONNECTICUT AVE. NW
202-842-3055 WWW.PROPERTOPPER.COM

RIZIK BROTHERS *CLOTHING*
Since 1908, Rizik's has supplied perfect (and pricey) outfits for crucial occasions – evening dresses, power suits, and wedding gowns – from both contemporary and classic designers.

MAP 5 D6 ⑨56 1100 CONNECTICUT AVE. NW
202-223-4050 WWW.RIZIKS.COM

SALON DANIEL *BATH, BEAUTY, AND SPA*
Young professionals, male and female, frequent this busy salon, which occupies a three-story townhouse. Hair, nail, and skin treatments are available, usually on the day you call.

MAP 5 C5 ⑨39 1831 ST. NW
202-296-4856

◖ SECOND STORY BOOKS & ANTIQUES *BOOKS*
A knowledgeable staff and an amazing collection of obscure, well-loved treasures (everything from old Hollywood to French lit) keep bookworms happy at this tiny, off-the-beaten-path hideaway.

MAP 5 B4 ⑨26 2000 P ST. NW
202-659-8884 WWW.SECONDSTORYBOOKS.COM

◖ TABLETOP *GIFT AND HOME*
The aesthetic at Tabletop is a cross between Andy Warhol and

Carol Brady. Retro modern reigns supreme here; funky lamps, curvy vases, and even handbags are among the whimsical wares.

MAP 5 A4 🛇4 1608 20TH ST. NW
202-387-7117 WWW.TABLETOPDC.COM

TINY JEWEL BOX *JEWELRY*

The owners of this D.C. institution search estate sales and work with designers to find one-of-a-kind pieces. Downstairs, ogle the expensive precious jewelry; upstairs, browse the modern, semi-precious, and faux pieces.

MAP 5 D6 🛇53 1147 CONNECTICUT AVE. NW
202-393-2747 WWW.TINYJEWELBOX.COM

TOAST AND STRAWBERRIES *CLOTHING*

Nothing here is mass-produced. Out-of-the-ordinary, bright clothing and decorative caftans are staples at this Dupont Circle boutique – one of the city's oldest black-owned stores.

MAP 5 A5 🛇11 1608 CONNECTICUT AVE. NW
202-234-1212 WWW.TOASTANDSTRAWBERRIES.COM

THE WRITTEN WORD *GIFT AND HOME*

Paper aficionados will love the handmade sheets and artistic greeting cards here. Fancy pens, luxurious ribbons, and custom letterpressed personal stationery are available, too.

MAP 5 B5 🛇32 1365 CONNECTICUT AVE. NW
202-223-1400 WWW.WRITTENWORDSTUDIO.COM

SHOPS

MAP 6 | 14TH AND U

ADC MAP AND TRAVEL CENTER *BOOKS*

Cartography galore is crammed into this tiny storefront. Plot your escape with detailed maps, globes, and National Geographic paraphernalia.

MAP 6 F2 🛇53 1636 I ST. NW
800-544-2659

CAKELOVE *GOURMET GOODIES*

The cakes at this cozy bakery are a cut above – impossibly rich and sinfully sugary. Lawyer-turned-baker Warren Brown has made such a name for himself that he's landed a sweet TV deal with the Food Network.

MAP 6 A3 🛇8 1506 U ST. NW
202-588-7100 WWW.CAKELOVE.COM

CANDIDA'S WORLD OF BOOKS *BOOKS*

This down-to-earth haven for bookworms specializes in writings from and about other cultures. Travel guides are plentiful here, also.

MAP 6 C3 🛇34 1541 14TH ST. NW
202-667-4811 OR 866-667-4811
WWW.CANDIDASWORLDOFBOOKS.COM

DA HSIN TRADING COMPANY *GIFT AND HOME*
Spot the shop by the huge Chinese vases in the window. Inside,
find a motley stock, including ceramic bowls of all sizes, inexpensive chopsticks, parasols, and beaded curtains.

MAP 6 F6 **S** 62   811 7TH ST. NW
202-789-4020

GARDEN DISTRICT *GIFT AND HOME*
This urban oasis is a lush escape from the grit of the city. Flowers,
plants, and greenery transport frazzled worker bees to a fragrant
paradise where spring is always in the air.

MAP 6 B3 **S** 26   1801 14TH ST. NW
202-797-9005   WWW.GARDENDISTRICT.BIZ

MULEH *GIFT AND HOME, CLOTHING*
Muleh doesn't just sell clothes and furniture, it presents a "lifestyle" that U Street habitués are eager to enjoy. Offbeat Asian
tables and chairs, the latest fashions from New York and Milan —
this is a one-stop shop for chic design and wardrobe.

MAP 6 B3 **S** 22   1831 14TH ST. NW
202-667-3440   WWW.MULEH.COM

NANA *CLOTHING, SHOES*
Nana deals in new and used, vintage and brand-name duds, along
with one-of-a-kind handbags and bath products, too. Members
Only jackets, Hobo bags, and Preloved constructions are all in the
mix here.

MAP 6 A2 **S** 4   1528 U ST. NW
202-667-6955   WWW.NANADC.COM

POP *CLOTHING*
Wacky apparel and modish accessories — fluorescent Penguin shirts,
retro Ben Sherman jeans, and limited edition watches and jewelry —
fly off the shelves at this candy-colored monument to pop culture.

MAP 6 B3 **S** 25   1803-A 14TH ST. NW
202-332-3312   WWW.SHOPPOP.COM

◖ U STREET *SHOPPING DISTRICT*
The epicenter of chic in D.C., "New U" is fast becoming a gentri-
fied haven for vintage clothing shops (Nana, Wild Women Wear
Red), urban furniture fixtures (Habitat, Home Rule), and sleek
boutiques (Maison 14, Pop).

MAP 6 A1 **S** 1   U ST. BTWN. 12TH AND 18TH STS. NW   WWW.14THANDU.ORG

VASTU *GIFT AND HOME*
Forget feng shui — Vastu is based on the ancient Sanskrit philosophy
that the placement of objects affects states of mind. Unconventional
furniture constructed by independent vendors is Vastu's calling
card, and 14th Street individualists appreciate the effort.

MAP 6 B3 **S** 23   1829 14TH ST. NW
202-234-8344   WWW.VASTUDC.COM

WILD WOMEN WEAR RED *CLOTHING, SHOES*
Sassy shoes and a smattering of cute clothes, plus orb-like stools
in a crimson room, lure window-shoppers inside. The prices are

often hefty, but the adorable mules, slides, heels, and sandals are guaranteed to soothe the sole.

`MAP 6` A2 Ⓢ5 1512 U ST. NW
202-387-5700 WWW.WILDWOMENWEARRED.COM

MAP 7 | UPPER NORTHWEST

SULLIVAN'S TOY STORE *KIDS STUFF*
Stocking both handmade and more mainstream toys, this cozy, family-owned spot is a great place to let kids' imaginations run wild.

`MAP 7` A2 Ⓢ1 3412 WISCONSIN AVE. NW
202-362-1343

VACE *GOURMET GOODIES*
Vace's succulent specialties are perfect for an Italian feast. After stocking up on authentic provisions such as homemade pizza dough and imported prosciutto, grab a crisp slice of pizza from the to-go counter.

`MAP 7` B6 Ⓢ13 3315 CONNECTICUT AVE. NW
202-363-1999

WAKE UP LITTLE SUZIE *GIFT AND HOME*
Pottery, jewelry, and glasswork fill this small Cleveland Park store. Objects range from small knickknacks and greeting cards to more expensive art pieces.

`MAP 7` A6 Ⓢ7 3409 CONNECTICUT AVE. NW
202-244-0700

MAP 8 | ADAMS MORGAN/WOODLEY PARK

BRASS KNOB ARCHITECTURAL ANTIQUES *ANTIQUES*
In addition to the many antique doorknobs, this shop also carries numerous antique light fixtures, stone accents, and other decorative hardware.

`MAP 8` D5 Ⓢ25 2311 18TH ST. NW
202-332-3370

THE DISTRICT LINE *CLOTHING*
Chipper service at fair prices is the hallmark of this no-frills Adams Morgan shop that specializes in labels from across the pond. Preppy polos mix and mingle with funky accessories for both lads and lasses.

`MAP 8` E5 Ⓢ29 2118 18TH ST. NW
202-558-5508 WWW.THEDISTRICTLINE.COM

18TH STREET *SHOPPING DISTRICT*
With shops and restaurants of every ethnic persuasion, this well-worn strip is the lifeblood of Adams Morgan. Culture vultures

share sidewalk space with fortune-tellers and street vendors as they peruse the edgy offerings.

MAP 8 **E5 S 31** 18TH ST. NW BTWN. SWANN AND CALVERT STS. NW
WWW.ADAMSMORGAN.NET

🌙 GINZA *GIFT AND HOME*
Traditional Japanese teacups, ornate dinnerware, sake carafes, and chopstick sets are displayed on wooden shelves in this Asian-themed store. There's a small collection of Japanese art and language books, too.

MAP 8 **F4 S 39** 1721 CONNECTICUT AVE. NW
202-331-7991   WWW.GINZAONLINE.COM

IDLE TIME BOOKS *BOOKS*
Idle Time is an earthy source for inexpensive, used books on every topic from Malaysian cooking to feminist literary criticism.

MAP 8 **C5 S 10** 2467 18TH ST. NW
202-232-4774   WWW.ABEBOOKS.COM/HOME/IDLETIME

MEEPS & AUNT NEENSIE'S FASHIONETTE *CLOTHING*
Orange leisure suits compete for hanger space next to pow-der-blue tuxedos in a Pepto-Bismol-hued room no bigger than Grandma's attic. Intrepid shoppers are often rewarded with vintage finds, perfect to wear out on the town – or to a Halloween party.

MAP 8 **E5 S 30** 2104 18TH ST. NW
202-265-6546   WWW.MEEPSONU.COM

SHAKE YOUR BOOTY *CLOTHING, SHOES*
Shop here for the latest in shoes and purses, in bright colors and this season's styles. The sale table makes it possible to score that great, cut-price find.

MAP 8 **D5 S 24** 2324 18TH ST. NW
202-518-8205

OFF MAP

POLITICS & PROSE BOOKSTORE
AND COFFEEHOUSE *BOOKS*
This intimate bookstore is a favorite among the Washington cognoscenti, who enjoy sipping espresso while browsing the great selection of political must-reads. High-profile events – Bill Clinton, Molly Ivins, Gary Hart – are an added bonus.

OFF MAP 5015 CONNECTICUT AVE. NW
202-364-1919   WWW.POLITICS-PROSE.COM

ARTS AND LEISURE

MUSEUMS AND GALLERIES

MAP 1 | WESTERN MALL/FOGGY BOTTOM

ART MUSEUM OF THE AMERICAS
The changing exhibitions here emphasize the art and culture of Latin America and the Caribbean. The museum's ornate Spanish colonial home features exterior iron grillwork and richly colored tiles.

MAP 1 C4 ◆ 37 201 18TH ST. NW
202-458-6016 WWW.MUSEUM.OAS.ORG

CORCORAN GALLERY OF ART
Among the treasures found in D.C.'s largest privately funded institution are Gilbert Stuart's famous portrait of George Washington and Frederic Church's stunning landscape, *Niagara*.

MAP 1 B5 ◆ 27 500 17TH ST. NW
202-639-1700 WWW.CORCORAN.ORG

DAUGHTERS OF THE AMERICAN REVOLUTION MUSEUM
Collecting quilts, plates, and other ephemera from the Revolution through the early 1900s, the D.A.R. Museum centers around historical reproductions of interior spaces. Among the 31 period rooms are a colonial parlor, a tavern, and a church.

MAP 1 C4 ◆ 36 1776 D ST. NW
202-628-1776 WWW.DAR.ORG

DECATUR HOUSE
Designed by America's first professional architect, Benjamin Henry Latrobe, this 1818 brick residence accommodated international dignitaries for more than a century. Museum collections include fine and decorative art from the period.

MAP 1 A5 ◆ 12 1610 H ST. NW (VISITOR'S ENTRANCE)
202-842-0920 WWW.DECATURHOUSE.ORG

RENWICK GALLERY
This Smithsonian museum displays the best in American crafts, paintings, and decorative arts of today and yesterday in an ornate French Second Empire–style building.

MAP 1 A5 ◆ 14 17TH ST. AND PENNSYLVANIA AVE. NW
202-633-2850
HTTP://AMERICANART.SI.EDU/RENWICK/INDEX.CFM

UNITED STATES DEPARTMENT OF THE INTERIOR MUSEUM
Exhibits highlight our government's role in Native American affairs, wildlife management, and geologic research. Be sure to

ALEXANDRIA: THE OTHER SIDE OF THE POTOMAC

Six miles away and almost 50 years older than the nation's capital, Alexandria is a must for any museum lover visiting Washington D.C. Located on the West bank of the Potomac, "Old Town" is charming with its authentic 18th-century buildings and cobblestone streets, yet the thriving city maintains a modern vibrancy with five-star restaurants and numerous art galleries. For a bit of history and art, visit the **Torpedo Factory Art Center** (105 N. Union St., 703-838-4565, www.torpedofactory.org), a renovated former munitions factory built during World War II and now home to more than 84 working studios and six galleries. Visitors are invited to join the artists in their studios while they work on painting, pottery, photography, jewelry, stained glass, printmaking, and more.

A visit to this side of the Potomac wouldn't be complete without a stop at George Washington's riverside estate, **Mount Vernon** (3200 Mount Vernon Memorial Hwy., Mount Vernon, VA, 703-780-2000, www.mountvernon.org), eight miles south of Alexandria. Here 500 acres of preserved colonial life awaits you. Afterward, return to Old Town to see where our founding fathers might have relaxed after a long day, at **Gadsby's Tavern Museum** (134 N. Royal St., 703-838-4242, http://oha.ci.alexandria.va.us/gadsby). Legend has it that this 1785 tavern and hotel is haunted.

walk around the grand 1930s-era Interior Building to admire its more than 25 murals and sculptures.

MAP 1 C4 ⭘ 34   1849 C ST. NW
202-208-4743   WWW.DOI.GOV/INTERIORMUSEUM

UNITED STATES HOLOCAUST MEMORIAL MUSEUM
See SIGHTS, p. 5.

MAP 1 D6 ⭘ 44   100 RAOUL WALLENBERG PL. SW
202-488-0400, 800-400-9373 (TIMED-ENTRY PASSES
FOR PERMANENT EXHIBITION HALL)   WWW.USHMM.ORG

MAP 2   SMITHSONIAN/PENN QUARTER

ARTHUR M. SACKLER GALLERY
The Sackler's Asian treasures include fine objects decorated with Chinese jade and an extensive collection of Islamic manuscripts.

ARTS AND LEISURE

INTERNATIONAL SPY MUSEUM

NATIONAL MUSEUM OF
NATURAL HISTORY

To see more works from the Far East, follow the gallery's underground passage to the Freer Gallery of Art.

MAP 2 E3 🅐 51 1050 INDEPENDENCE AVE. SW
202-633-4880 WWW.ASIA.SI.EDU

🄲 DONALD W. REYNOLDS CENTER FOR AMERICAN ART AND PORTRAITURE

After a much-anticipated 6.5-year renovation, the Smithsonian American Art Museum and the National Portrait Gallery reopened in July 2006 in the old Patent Office Building. Telling the American story through portraits of people that shaped the country and artworks that depict the American experience, the museums are no longer two separate entities: They alternate floors over four stories, with most of the pieces organized chronologically. Among them, you'll find new faces like Hillary Clinton and Shaquille O'Neal along with iconic pieces, like Edward Hopper's *Cape Cod Morning*. One of the most original additions is the Lunder Conservation Center, where visitors can watch conservators preserving masterpieces in glassed-in workshops.

MAP 2 B4 🅐 20 8TH AND F STS. NW
202-633-1000 HTTP://REYNOLDSCENTER.ORG

FREER GALLERY OF ART

Displaying masterpieces in a beautiful Italian Renaissance–style building, this Smithsonian museum and the Sackler Gallery together form the National Museum of Asian Art.

MAP 2 E3 🅐 50 JEFFERSON DR. AT 12TH ST. SW
202-633-4880 WWW.ASIA.SI.EDU

HIRSHHORN MUSEUM AND SCULPTURE GARDEN

Visit the Hirshhorn, the Smithsonian's modern art space, for impressive works by Henry Moore, Picasso, and Rodin, but especially for art created in the last 30 years.

MAP 2 E4 🅐 53 7TH ST. AND INDEPENDENCE AVE. SW
202-633-4674 HTTP://HIRSHHORN.SI.EDU

🄲 INTERNATIONAL SPY MUSEUM

Interactive multimedia presentations, photography, and artifacts provide a historical examination of espionage around the world. Highlights include a collection of eye-popping spy gadgetry and film interviews with former CIA and KGB agents. Same-day and advance tickets can be purchased in the lobby; advance tickets can be purchased through Ticketmaster, too.

MAP 2 B4 ⓐ21 800 F ST. NW
202-393-7798   WWW.SPYMUSEUM.ORG

MARIAN KOSHLAND SCIENCE MUSEUM
The official museum of the National Academy of Sciences strives to illuminate the pertinent scientific topics of today with interactive and engaging exhibits such as "Global Warming Facts and Our Future" and "Putting DNA to Work."

MAP 2 B5 ⓐ26 6TH AND E ST. NW
202-334-1201 OR 888-567-4526
WWW.KOSHLAND-SCIENCE-MUSEUM.ORG

NATIONAL AIR AND SPACE MUSEUM
See SIGHTS, p. 9.

MAP 2 E5 ⊕54 INDEPENDENCE AVE. AND 4TH ST. SW
202-633-1000   WWW.NASM.SI.EDU

NATIONAL ARCHIVES
See SIGHTS, p. 10.

MAP 2 D4 ⊕44 CONSTITUTION AVE. BTWN. 7TH AND 9TH STS. NW
866-272-6272
WWW.ARCHIVES.GOV/DC-METRO/WASHINGTON

NATIONAL BUILDING MUSEUM
Stretching more than 300 feet in length and incorporating eight gigantic Corinthian columns, the museum's Great Hall is the main attraction here, but don't miss the thought-provoking exhibits on modern architecture.

MAP 2 B6 ⓐ27 401 F ST. NW
202-272-2448   WWW.NBM.ORG

NATIONAL GALLERY OF ART
See SIGHTS, p. 11.

MAP 2 D5 ⊕46 CONSTITUTION AVE. NW BTWN. 4TH AND 7TH STS. NW
202-737-4215   WWW.NGA.GOV

NATIONAL MUSEUM OF AFRICAN ART
Located underground in the Smithsonian Quadrangle complex, this museum's permanent collection of approximately 8,000 items, which include photographs, masks, jewelry, and carvings, will enhance your understanding of African cultures.

MAP 2 E3 ⓐ52 950 INDEPENDENCE AVE. SW
202-633-4600   WWW.NMAFA.SI.EDU

NATIONAL MUSEUM OF NATURAL HISTORY
The nation's largest research museum is filled with fossils, plants, animals, and gems: The collections include more than 125 million specimens, although not all of them are on display. The Hope Diamond is on permanent exhibition.

MAP 2 D3 ⓐ43 10TH ST. AND CONSTITUTION AVE. NW
202-633-1000   WWW.MNH.SI.EDU

NATIONAL MUSEUM OF THE AMERICAN INDIAN
Opened in September 2004, this third branch of the NMAI highlights Native American culture and achievement. Permanent

ARTS AND LEISURE

exhibits focus on worldviews, peoples, and contemporary issues; theme- or artist-based shows comprise the temporary offerings.

MAP 2 E6 ⊘55 4TH ST. AND INDEPENDENCE AVE. SW
202-633-1000 WWW.NMAI.SI.EDU

SMITHSONIAN INSTITUTION
See SIGHTS, p. 12.

MAP 2 E3 ⊘49 1000 JEFFERSON DR. SW
202-633-1000 WWW.SI.EDU

U.S. NAVY MEMORIAL AND NAVAL HERITAGE CENTER
Come search the computers for records of your favorite Navy veteran. Afterward, an exciting short film, *At Sea,* will put you aboard a modern aircraft carrier.

MAP 2 C4 ⊘40 701 PENNSYLVANIA AVE. NW
202-737-2300 OR 800-821-8892 WWW.LONESAILOR.ORG

◖ ZENITH GALLERY
Founded in 1978 and located in Penn Quarter's rapidly growing arts district, Zenith is one of the most eclectic private galleries in Washington, offering a contemporary collection that includes sculptures, ceramics, glass, and neon art.

MAP 2 C4 ⊘34 413 7TH ST. NW
202-783-2963 WWW.ZENITHGALLERY.COM

MAP 3 CAPITOL HILL

FOLGER SHAKESPEARE LIBRARY
This award-winning neoclassical building with art deco details is home to the world's largest collection of works by and about the Bard. Most of the works are available only to researchers, but the concerts, lectures, and performances are open to all.

MAP 3 E4 ⊘18 201 E. CAPITOL ST. SE
202-544-4600 WWW.FOLGER.EDU

NATIONAL POSTAL MUSEUM
An enormous collection of stamps and three vintage mail planes are among the interesting exhibits that put a unique spin on U.S. postal history.

MAP 3 B2 ⊘1 2 MASSACHUSETTS AVE. NE
202-633-5555 WWW.POSTALMUSEUM.SI.EDU

MAP 4 GEORGETOWN

◖ DUMBARTON OAKS
Harvard University maintains the excellent collection of paintings, rare books, Byzantine coins, and pre-Columbian artifacts in this expansive 19th-century home, which reopens in 2007 after a

DUMBARTON OAKS   THE OLD STONE HOUSE

renovation. Outside, 10 acres of gardens remain open and are a treat year-round.

MAP 4 B4 ○4 1703 32ND ST. NW
202-339-6401 WWW.DOAKS.ORG

FINE ART & ARTISTS GALLERY

This three-story row house is devoted to pop and contemporary masters, including Lichtenstein, Warhol, and Rauschenberg. A courtyard garden features rotating exhibits by contemporary artists.

MAP 4 E6 ○36 2920 M ST. NW
202-965-0780 WWW.FAAGALLERY.COM

GOVINDA GALLERY

Annie Leibovitz had her first D.C. show here in 1984, kicking off the gallery's well-earned reputation as a mainstay for rock 'n' roll photography.

MAP 4 E3 ○15 1227 34TH ST. NW
202-333-1180 WWW.GOVINDAGALLERY.COM

THE OLD STONE HOUSE

Tucked into Georgetown's busiest shopping street, this original 18th-century home is a window into simpler times, with mostly original furnishings on display in six colonial-style rooms. The large backyard garden is a breathtaking surprise. Group tours are by reservation only.

MAP 4 E5 ○30 3051 M ST. NW
202-895-6070 WWW.NPS.GOV/OLST

MAP 5 DUPONT CIRCLE

ALEX GALLERY

Occupying three full floors, this is one of the largest galleries in Dupont Circle and features contemporary paintings and sculptures by American and European artists.

MAP 5 A4 ○1 2106 R ST. NW
202-667-2599 WWW.ALEXGALLERIES.COM

ARTS AND LEISURE

KATHLEEN EWING GALLERY
A D.C. art institution, this gallery displays vintage and contemporary photography in a friendly, apartment-like atmosphere.

MAP 5 A5 ⓐ9 1609 CONNECTICUT AVE. NW
202-328-0955   WWW.KATHLEENEWINGGALLERY.COM

THE PHILLIPS COLLECTION
Started as just two rooms in the Phillips family's personal residence, the nation's first modern art museum is also one of Washington's most beautiful spaces. Diebenkorns, Mondrians, Rothkos, and the like comprise this fine collection.

MAP 5 A4 ⓐ3 1600 21ST ST. NW
202-387-2151   WWW.PHILLIPSCOLLECTION.ORG

THE SOCIETY OF THE CINCINNATI
The Beaux-Arts mansion of the society (which also claims George Washington as its first president) contains a large collection of European and Asian fine art and antiques, as well as artifacts from the American Revolution.

MAP 5 B4 ⓐ16 2118 MASSACHUSETTS AVE. NW
202-785-2040
WWW.THESOCIETYOFTHECINCINNATI.ADDR.COM

ⓒ SPECTRUM GALLERY
Founded in 1966 by local artists, the original offerings at this artist-owned gallery include paintings, photography, prints, and sculpture. Two exhibitions rotate monthly: a featured exhibition and a group show of all the artists represented by the gallery.

MAP 5 B3 ⓐ15 1421 22ND ST. NW
202-833-1616   WWW.SPECTRUMGALLERY.ORG

MAP 6 | 14TH AND U

IRVINE CONTEMPORARY
Striking a good balance between the popular (colorful drawings) and avant-garde (TV screens flashing hypnotic linear designs), this gallery appeals to a wide range of contemporary art fans.

MAP 6 D3 ⓐ41 1412 14TH ST. NW
202-332-8767   HTTP://IRVINECONTEMPORARY.COM

MARY MCLEOD BETHUNE COUNCIL HOUSE
Formerly the headquarters of the National Council of Negro Women, this restored 19th-century townhouse now houses a museum dedicated to Bethune, who founded the NCNW, as well as the National Archives for Black Women's History.

MAP 6 D4 ⓐ43 1318 VERMONT AVE. NW
202-673-2402   WWW.NPS.GOV/MAMC

THE NATIONAL GEOGRAPHIC MUSEUM
AT EXPLORERS HALL
Interactive displays put the society's wealth of knowledge at your

fingertips, and a small gallery showcases a new world-class photography exhibit every month.

 E2 ⚓ 46 1145 17TH ST. NW
202-857-7588
WWW.NATIONALGEOGRAPHIC.COM/MUSEUM

NATIONAL MUSEUM OF WOMEN IN THE ARTS

At the only museum to exclusively exhibit the works of women artists, the mixed-media collections include lesser-knowns as well as superstars such as Georgia O'Keeffe, Mary Cassatt, and Frida Kahlo.

MAP 6 F4 ⚓ 59 1250 NEW YORK AVE. NW
202-783-5000 OR 800-222-7270   WWW.NMWA.ORG

TRANSFORMER GALLERY

Inside a somewhat nondescript row house near Logan Circle, this nonprofit art space showcases local and emerging mixed-media artists. Expect the avant-garde exhibits, which include sound and video installations, to challenge your perceptions of art.

MAP 6 C3 ⚓ 38 1404 P ST. NW
202-483-1102   WWW.TRANSFORMERGALLERY.ORG

MAP 8 | ADAMS MORGAN/WOODLEY PARK

ARTS AND LEISURE

CONNER CONTEMPORARY ART

Whether it's abstract sculpture, colorful pop art, contemporary photography, or digital media, the work shown in this small gallery's monthly exhibits is always some of the most original in Washington.

MAP 8 F4 ⚓ 38 1730 CONNECTICUT AVE. NW, 2ND FL.
202-588-8750   WWW.CONNERCONTEMPORARY.COM

DISTRICT OF COLUMBIA ARTS CENTER

A cornerstone of the Washington arts scene, DCAC exhibits the work of local artists, including metallic sculptures, mixed-media paintings, and video performance art. The black-box theater features films, plays, and improv comedy.

MAP 8 D5 ⚓ 18 2438 18TH ST. NW
202-462-7833   WWW.DCARTSCENTER.ORG

THE TEXTILE MUSEUM

Inside the museum's two elegant townhouses are pre-Columbian, Egyptian, and Islamic textiles and a fine collection of Peruvian weavings, although displays may be limited when there's no marquee exhibit.

MAP 8 F3 ⚓ 34 2320 S ST. NW
202-667-0441   WWW.TEXTILEMUSEUM.ORG

WOODROW WILSON HOUSE

Our 28th president chose this elegant brick townhouse for his retirement after leaving the White House. On display are trophies and souvenirs of his presidency.

MAP 8 F3 ⓐ 33 2340 S ST. NW
202-387-4062 WWW.WOODROWWILSONHOUSE.ORG

OVERVIEW MAP

HILLWOOD MUSEUM AND GARDENS
The glamorous home of cereal heiress Marjorie Merriweather Post is filled with rare decorative arts and furniture collections, which includes two imperial Fabergé Easter eggs, and sits on a 25-acre estate complete with cultivated gardens overlooking Rock Creek Park. Reservations are required.

OVERVIEW MAP A4 4155 LINNEAN AVE. NW
202-686-5807 OR 877-445-5966
WWW.HILLWOODMUSEUM.ORG

PERFORMING ARTS

MAP 1 | **WESTERN MALL/FOGGY BOTTOM**

DAR CONSTITUTION HALL *MUSIC*

Every president since Calvin Coolidge has attended an event at Constitution Hall. A variety of superstars, from pop music's Bruce Springsteen to opera's Cecelia Bartoli, has taken the stage of this giant neoclassical venue.

MAP 1 C4🅐35   311 18TH ST. NW
202-628-4780   WWW.DAR.ORG/CONTHALL

DOROTHY BETTS MARVIN THEATRE *VARIOUS*

Located in George Washington University's Marvin Center, this campus theater stages professional performances by the university's theater, music, and dance departments year-round.

MAP 1 A3🅐4   MARVIN CENTER, 800 21ST ST. NW
202-994-7470   HTTP://GWIRED.GWU.EDU/MARVINCENTER

EISENHOWER THEATER *VARIOUS*

Part of the Kennedy Center complex, the 1,100-seat Eisenhower brings in surprises and star power with its array of contemporary dance, ballet, musicals, and other theatrical works.

MAP 1 B1🅐19   KENNEDY CENTER, 2700 F ST. NW
202-467-4600 OR 202-416-8000
WWW.KENNEDY-CENTER.ORG

 JOHN F. KENNEDY CENTER FOR THE PERFORMING ARTS *VARIOUS*

Ever since it opened in the early '70s, the Kennedy Center has anchored the performing arts scene in D.C. The center's five theaters present an ever-changing mix of offerings, including opera, music festivals, plays, dance, and musicals.

MAP 1 B1🅐18   2700 F ST. NW
202-416-8000 OR 800-444-1324
WWW.KENNEDY-CENTER.ORG

KENNEDY CENTER CONCERT HALL *MUSIC*

The largest of the Kennedy Center auditoriums, the concert hall is home to the National Symphony Orchestra. State-of-the-art acoustics, crystal chandeliers, and plush seating make for a premier concert experience.

MAP 1 B1🅐24   KENNEDY CENTER, 2700 F ST. NW
202-467-4600 OR 202-416-8000
WWW.KENNEDY-CENTER.ORG

KENNEDY CENTER OPERA HOUSE *OPERA*

The Washington National Opera, under the direction of Plàcido

ARTS AND LEISURE

Domingo, mounts beautiful productions in this 2,300-seat house. It is also the opulent setting for dance extravaganzas and large-scale musicals.

MAP 1 B1 ⓐ 20   KENNEDY CENTER, 2700 F ST. NW
202-295-2400 OR 202-416-8000
WWW.KENNEDY-CENTER.ORG

LISNER AUDITORIUM   *MUSIC*
The eclectic roster at this George Washington University theater runs the gamut from jazz great Quincy Jones to Engelbert Humperdinck to Buddhist musical festivals.

MAP 1 A3 ⓐ 5   730 21ST ST. NW
202-994-6800   WWW.LISNER.ORG

MILLENNIUM STAGE   *MUSIC*
This stage in the Kennedy Center's Grand Foyer brings art to the masses with free performances (mostly musical, with occasional comedy, dance, and readings) daily at 6 P.M. No tickets are required; just show up – the earlier the better.

MAP 1 B1 ⓐ 21   KENNEDY CENTER, 2700 F ST. NW
202-467-4600 OR 202-416-8000
WWW.KENNEDY-CENTER.ORG

SYLVAN THEATER   *MUSIC*
This outdoor theater on the Washington Monument grounds comes alive in the summer with free concerts by military bands and the National Symphony Orchestra.

MAP 1 D6 ⓐ 43   NATIONAL MALL AT 15TH ST. AND CONSTITUTION AVE. NW
202-619-7222

TERRACE THEATER   *THEATER*
The Philip Johnson–designed Terrace Theater presents chamber recitals as well as dramatic and experimental plays in its small, 513-seat space.

MAP 1 B1 ⓐ 22   KENNEDY CENTER, 2700 F ST. NW
202-416-8000   WWW.KENNEDY-CENTER.ORG

THEATER LAB   *THEATER*
Known as the home of *Shear Madness,* an audience-participation suspense comedy about a murder in a beauty salon, the Theater Lab focuses primarily on programs for young people.

MAP 1 B1 ⓐ 23   KENNEDY CENTER, 2700 F ST. NW
202-467-4600 OR 800-444-1324
WWW.KENNEDYCENTER.ORG

MAP 2   SMITHSONIAN/PENN QUARTER

CAPITOL STEPS   *COMEDY*
This troupe with many current and former congressional staffers puts its own spin on the political world with hilarious spoofs and satirical songs every Friday and Saturday night.

MAP 2 B2 ⓐ 13   RONALD REAGAN BUILDING AND INTERNATIONAL TRADE
CENTER AMPHITHEATER, 1300 PENNSYLVANIA AVE. NW
202-312-1555   WWW.CAPSTEPS.COM

NATIONAL THEATRE   THE SHAKESPEARE THEATRE

FORD'S THEATRE *THEATER*

History buffs flock to see where Abe Lincoln sat the night he was assassinated. Despite its violent past, Ford's productions are strictly family fare.

MAP 2 B3 **16** 511 10TH ST. NW
202-638-2941 OR 202-347-4833
WWW.FORDSTHEATRE.ORG

LANDMARK'S E STREET CINEMA *MOVIE HOUSE*

Enjoy an espresso while watching the latest independent, foreign, and documentary films. This indie movie house boasts Dolby Digital sound and stadium seating in seven of its eight theaters.

MAP 2 B3 **15** 555 11TH ST. NW
202-452-7672   WWW.LANDMARKTHEATRES.COM

NATIONAL THEATRE *THEATER*

Washington's take on 42nd Street, this 1835 landmark theater mounts full-scale Broadway hits – mostly musicals like *Chicago* and *Show Boat,* with the occasional drama. It also offers free shows and a film from time to time – call for a schedule.

MAP 2 B2 **11** 1321 PENNSYLVANIA AVE. NW
202-628-6161   WWW.NATIONALTHEATRE.ORG

THE SHAKESPEARE THEATRE *THEATER*

This intimate 451-seat venue is counted among the finest performance spaces in the city. Under Michael Kahn's direction, the theater presents internationally acclaimed productions of works by Shakespeare and other classic playwrights.

MAP 2 C4 **32** 450 7TH ST. NW
202-547-1122   WWW.SHAKESPEAREDC.ORG

VERIZON CENTER *MUSIC*

The home of D.C.'s own basketball and hockey teams, this 20,000-seat downtown arena is where the likes of U2 and the Rolling Stones perform when they come to town.

MAP 2 B5 **25** 601 F ST. NW
202-628-3200   WWW.VERIZONCENTER.COM

WARNER THEATRE *VARIOUS*

Enjoy comedy, drama, jazz, or even a circus in the restored

ARTS AND LEISURE

FOLGER THEATRE

WOOLLY MAMMOTH
THEATRE COMPANY

elegance of this former 1920s movie house. The lobby bar opens a half-hour before showtime.

MAP 2 B2 ⓐ12   513 13TH ST. NW
202-783-4000   WWW.WARNERTHEATRE.COM

◖ WASHINGTON IMPROV THEATER   *COMEDY*

Using audience suggestions and free-form unscripted comedy, this professional theater troupe never ceases to shock and surprise. The troupe performs regularly at their home theater, Flashpoint, as well as at local and national festivals.

MAP 2 A4 ⓐ6   FLASHPOINT, 916 G ST. NW
202-315-1318   WWW.WASHINGTONIMPROVTHEATER.COM

WOOLLY MAMMOTH THEATRE COMPANY   *THEATER*

Living up to its reputation as Washington's "most daring theater company," the Woolly Mammoth stages groundbreaking performances such as *The Faculty Room* and *Dead Man's Cell Phone* in its 265-seat contemporary basement theater.

MAP 2 C4 ⓐ39   614 D ST. NW
202-289-2443   WWW.WOOLLYMAMMOTH.NET

MAP 3 | CAPITOL HILL

COOLIDGE AUDITORIUM   *MUSIC*

The excellent acoustics in this intimate Library of Congress hall enhance the considerable talents of the visiting chamber groups, string quartets, and, occasionally, soloists from the National Symphony Orchestra.

MAP 3 E4 ⓐ17   101 INDEPENDENCE AVE. SE
202-707-5502   WWW.LOC.GOV/CONCERTS

FOLGER THEATRE   *THEATER*

Shakespeare himself would surely approve of this 250-seat Elizabethan playhouse, with its three tiers of wooden balconies and a canopy painted to replicate the sky. The three-play season includes performances of Shakespeare's plays, as well as contemporary works inspired by the bard.

MAP 3 E4 ⓐ19   FOLGER SHAKESPEARE LIBRARY, 201 E. CAPITOL ST. SE
202-544-7077   WWW.FOLGER.EDU

AFI SILVER THEATRE

If you're ever going to go outside the District for a movie, make sure that it's at the American Film Institute's Silver Theatre and Cultural Center (8633 Colesville Rd., Silver Spring, MD, 301-495-6720, www.afi.com/silver). With its unmistakable glowing marquee, this movie house was refurbished from a classic 1938 theater that was once nearly demolished. It is now the D.C.-area outpost of the American Film Institute, a national organization dedicated to the moving image. It showcases a variety of foreign films, documentaries, and classics on its three screens, as well as hosts numerous special events, such as the SilverDocs film festival. In addition, it's almost easier to get to than some in-town neighborhoods: Just take the Metro Red Line one stop outside D.C. to Silver Spring, and it's two blocks north of the station.

MAP 4 | GEORGETOWN

DUMBARTON CHURCH CONCERTS *MUSIC*
Washington's best chamber music – classical, jazz, and early music – is presented in historic Dumbarton Church October–April. Concerts are candlelit for added ambience.

MAP 4 D5 ⓐ11   3133 DUMBARTON ST. NW
202-965-2000   WWW.DUMBARTONCONCERTS.ORG

MAP 6 | 14TH AND U

HR-57 CENTER FOR THE PRESERVATION OF JAZZ AND BLUES *MUSIC*
By day, this neighborhood cultural center hosts workshops and classes on jazz and blues. At night, some of the area's best musicians illustrate how it's done. You can BYOB for a small corkage fee.

MAP 6 C3 ⓐ33   1610 14TH ST. NW
202-667-3700   WWW.HR57.ORG

LINCOLN THEATRE *VARIOUS*
The Lincoln Theatre recalls the heyday of the historic U Street district. From comedy shows to gospel performances, this magnificently restored 1920s theater venue features a diverse spectrum of entertainment.

MAP 6 A4 ⓐ15   1215 U ST. NW
202-328-6000   WWW.THELINCOLNTHEATRE.ORG

ALL OF D.C.'S A STAGE

And we are but its audience, enjoying the many outdoor performances on warm summer evenings. On Monday nights in July and August, **Screen on the Green** (877-262-5866) shows classic films at sunset on the Mall, between 4th and 7th Streets NW. At the opposite end of the week, the **Sculpture Garden at the National Gallery (p. 84)** hosts Jazz in the Garden every Friday night, 5–8:30 P.M., late May–mid-September. Off the Mall, Rock Creek Park's **Carter Barron Amphitheatre** (16th St. and Colorado Ave. NW, 202-426-0486, www.nps.gov/rocr) kicks off the summer season with a weeklong run of the **Shakespeare Theatre's (p. 77)** "Free for All," free, ticketed performances of the Bard. **Wolf Trap, the National Park for the Performing Arts** (1551 Trap Rd., Vienna, VA, 703-255-1900, www.wolftrap.org) offers a great excuse for a jaunt outside the city, with summer theatrical, dance, and concert performances in its outdoor amphitheatre. The best seats are on the lawn, where you can relax with a picnic (including alcoholic beverages).

STUDIO THEATRE *THEATER*

With its 2004 expansion, this contemporary theater now includes the space of two former 1920s automobile showrooms. Expect bold performances of U.S. and European works.

MAP **6** C3 **◊** 37 1501 14TH ST. NW
202-332-3300   WWW.STUDIOTHEATRE.ORG

THEATER J/AARON AND
CECILE GOLDMAN THEATER *VARIOUS*

Theater J performs an American-Jewish repertoire in the elegant 236-seat Aaron and Cecile Goldman Theater. The multifaceted space frequently plays host to music and film festivals, too.

MAP **6** C2 **◊** 28 1529 16TH ST. NW
202-518-9400   WWW.DCJCC.ORG/ARTS/THEATERJ

WAREHOUSE *VARIOUS*

D.C.'s edgiest and most bare-bones arts complex began as a gallery in 1995 and now includes two black-box theaters, a screening room, space for live music, and a café.

MAP **6** E6 **◊** 50 1017-1021 7TH ST. NW
202-783-3933   WWW.WAREHOUSETHEATER.COM

MAP 7 | UPPER NORTHWEST

◖ LOEWS CINEPLEX ODEON UPTOWN *MOVIE HOUSE*
Among the last of a dying breed, this classic movie house boasts one – yes, only one – big screen, perfect for viewing the special-effects blockbuster of the moment. Arrive early for a coveted balcony seat.

MAP 7 A6 **◬** 9 3426 CONNECTICUT AVE. NW
202-966-8805

OVERVIEW MAP

ARENA STAGE *THEATER*
Founded in 1950, the internationally renowned Arena Stage presents new and classic American theater in its three venues: the in-the-round Fichandler Stage, the proscenium-shaped Kreeger, and the intimate Old Vat Room.

OVERVIEW MAP E5 1101 6TH ST. SW
202-488-3300   WWW.ARENASTAGE.ORG

CAPITOL HILL ARTS WORKSHOP *MOVIE HOUSE*
This amateur film society shows classic movies from the 1910s through the 1950s. A piano accompaniment jazzes up the silent movies.

OVERVIEW MAP E6 545 7TH ST. SE
202-547-6839   WWW.CHAW.ORG

GALA HISPANIC THEATRE *THEATER*
After 29 years, GALA has found a permanent home at the historic and recently renovated Tivoli Theatre. Latin culture is celebrated in musicals, art exhibitions, lectures, and more, with easy-to-follow projected subtitles.

OVERVIEW MAP B4 2437 15TH ST. NW
202-234-7174   WWW.GALATHEATRE.ORG

ARTS AND LEISURE

RECREATION

MAP 1 | WESTERN MALL/FOGGY BOTTOM

CITY SEGWAY TOURS
After a quick tutorial, you'll be cruising down city sidewalks aboard a Segway on a four-hour guided tour of Washington's monuments and memorials. Opt for the night tour, which starts at 6 P.M., to watch dusk settle over the city as the monument lights illuminate the Mall.

MAP 1 B6 ● 29   PENNSYLVANIA AVE. NW BTWN. WILLARD INTERCONTINENTAL AND HOTEL WASHINGTON
877-734-8687   WWW.CITYSEGWAYTOUR.COM/WASHINGTON

LADY BIRD JOHNSON PARK/ LYNDON B. JOHNSON MEMORIAL GROVE
Lady Bird Johnson Park is a beautifully landscaped tribute to a woman who contributed much to outdoor beauty, with 17 acres of winding trails and a memorial grove of pine and dogwood trees honoring our 36th president.

MAP 1 F1 ● 49   GEORGE WASHINGTON PKWY. AT ARLINGTON MEMORIAL BRIDGE (VIRGINIA)
703-289-2500

LAFAYETTE SQUARE
Mingle with presidential staffers on lunch in this elegant and formal D.C. park. Its location across from the White House also makes this public space a favorite of outspoken protesters.

MAP 1 A5 ● 13   H ST. NW BTWN. JACKSON PL. NW AND E. EXECUTIVE AVE.
202-426-6841

PERSHING PARK
At this downtown oasis, you can feed ducks at the pond, grab a snack, and watch the world go by; in winter, there's also ice-skating. A circus of skateboarders typically flocks to adjacent Freedom Plaza.

MAP 1 B6 ● 31   14TH ST. AND PENNSYLVANIA AVE. NW
202-737-6938

TIDAL BASIN BOATHOUSE
Paddleboats are available to rent March–October. Tone up those calf muscles – or let your partner do all the work – while taking in the Jefferson Memorial and the spring cherry blossoms.

MAP 1 E6 ● 47   1501 MAINE AVE. SW
202-479-2426

◖ WEST POTOMAC PARK
This ethereal park is the setting for the Lincoln Memorial, the

World War II Memorial, the Reflecting Pool, and the famous Japanese cherry trees that bloom around the Tidal Basin each spring.

 E3 Ⓐ45 WEST OF 17TH ST. NW AND
SOUTH OF CONSTITUTION AVE. NW
202-426-6841

MAP 2 | SMITHSONIAN/PENN QUARTER

BIKE THE SITES
Explore Washington's monuments, museums, and memorials on a guided three-hour bike tour. Night tours and cherry blossom tours are also offered, and the company rents bikes out if you prefer to be your own guide.

MAP 2 C3 Ⓐ31 1100 PENNSYLVANIA AVE. NW
202-842-2453 WWW.BIKETHESITES.COM

NATIONAL MALL
A green expanse bordered by the Smithsonian museums, the Capitol, and various monuments, the Mall is the city's playground, where everyone is welcome and anything can unfold, from pick-up soccer games and free concerts to pro-choice protests and military parades.

MAP 2 E3 Ⓐ48 BTWN. CONSTITUTION AND INDEPENDENCE AVES.,
THE CAPITOL AND LINCOLN MEMORIAL
202-426-6841

ARTS AND LEISURE

BEACH DRIVE

On weekends and holidays, the National Park Service closes Beach Drive, a rolling, two-lane road that slices through the narrow, 1,755-acre **Rock Creek National Park (p. 87),** to motorized traffic. From 7 A.M. until 7 P.M., hikers, cyclists, inline skaters, joggers, and families with strollers take over this scenic stretch of asphalt. You can picnic alongside the creek, barbecue at designated spots, or sweat off last night's long night out by jogging on the road or exploring miles of hiking trails that snake into the park. Historic **Peirce Mill** (Tilden Street at Beach Dr., 202-895-6070), also part of Rock Creek Park, offers free parking and easy access to Beach Drive. The sections of Beach Drive that close to traffic include from Broad Branch Road to Military Road, from Picnic Grove 10 to Wise Road, and from West Beach Drive to the D.C.–Maryland border.

SCULPTURE GARDEN AT THE NATIONAL GALLERY OF ART

World-class contemporary art and beautiful landscaping surround a lively public rink, open for ice-skating November–March. A small café makes it a great spot to refresh when museum fatigue strikes.

MAP 2 D4 ⓐ45   BTWN. 7TH AND 9TH STS. NW, CONSTITUTION AVE. AND MADISON DR. NW
202-737-4215   WWW.NGA.GOV

MAP 3 | CAPITOL HILL

◖ BARTHOLDI FOUNTAIN AND PARK

Named for sculptor and Statue of Liberty designer Frederic Auguste Bartholdi, the elaborate fountain is the centerpiece of this fantastic flower-filled space opposite the U.S. Botanical Garden.

MAP 3 E1 ⓐ15   1ST ST. AND INDEPENDENCE AVE. SW

D.C. DUCKS

For an off-the-beaten-path experience, tour the city's streets and waterways on this restored World War II amphibious truck. The 90-minute tours are offered mid-March–October.

MAP 3 B3 ⓐ6   UNION STATION, 50 MASSACHUSETTS AVE. NE
202-832-9800

OLD TOWN TROLLEY TOURS

Boarding at Union Station, this two-hour narrated tour of the city on a trolley-shaped bus will hit more than 100 highlights, with plenty of stops along the way.

MAP 3 B3 ⓐ7   UNION STATION, 50 MASSACHUSETTS AVE. NE
202-966-3825

MAP 4 | GEORGETOWN

CHESAPEAKE & OHIO CANAL NATIONAL HISTORICAL PARK

At this historic park, you can take a one-hour mule-drawn boat ride up the C & O canal, April–October. Rangers dressed in period clothing tell stories and sing ballads along the way. Walking tours are also available.

MAP 4 F5 ⓐ41   VISITORS CENTER, 1057 THOMAS JEFFERSON ST. NW
202-653-5190

CHESAPEAKE & OHIO CANAL TOWPATH

This flat hiking and biking trail meanders alongside the Potomac for 184.5 miles, becoming increasingly scenic the farther you go. If you hike 14 miles (one-way), you'll be rewarded with views of a spectacular waterfall.

MAP 4 F5 ⓐ40   VISITORS CENTER, 1057 THOMAS JEFFERSON ST. NW
202-653-5190

ARTS AND LEISURE

BARTHOLDI FOUNTAIN AND PARK   *THE EXORCIST* STAIRS   WASHINGTON HARBOUR

DUMBARTON OAKS PARK

Enter this 27-acre park through grand wrought-iron gates situated on a residential street. The path grows wilder as it meanders alongside Rock Creek.

MAP 4 A4 **1**   ENTER AT 31ST AND R STS. NW
202-426-6841

THE EXORCIST STAIRS

This 75-step (five-story) stairway – the location of the priest's fall in the famous movie – offers a dizzying descent down to M Street shops and eateries. Today, Georgetown athletes train by running the steps.

MAP 4 E2 **13**   36TH AND PROSPECT STS. NW

JACK'S BOATHOUSE

Rent canoes and kayaks from this seldom-visited D.C. institution, in operation since 1945. Ply the waters of the Potomac for an hour or an entire day. Call ahead to arrange for a tour.

MAP 4 F3 **38**   3500 K ST. NW
202-337-9642   WWW.JACKSBOATHOUSE.COM

MONTROSE PARK

During the 19th century, rope-making magnate Robert Parrott generously allowed his land to be used for local meetings and picnics. Today, the park's gardens, picnic tables, tennis courts, and 16 acres of rugged trails belong to the grateful citizenry of Georgetown.

MAP 4 B5 **5**   30TH AND R STS. NW

WASHINGTON HARBOUR

A bustling mix of residences, marinas, shops, and restaurants keeps this stretch of waterfront hopping year-round. Enjoy excellent people-watching opportunities and panoramic views across the Potomac.

MAP 4 F5 **43**   31ST AND K STS. NW

ARTS AND LEISURE

STEP INTO THE PAST

To travel beyond the typical tourist circuit – and to gain a greater appreciation for D.C.'s diverse cultural history – spend an afternoon traversing one of the city's six Neighborhood Heritage Trails, introduced in 2005. These self-guided walks follow a series of illustrated signs to unveil the background of different D.C. locales, from the story of greater U Street's once-thriving African American community to the history of D.C.'s waterfront to Capitol Hill's military and political past. The points on each trail are arranged chronologically, but you can dip in and out of the route at your leisure, stopping at cafés and shops that line much of the routes. The trails' organizer, **Cultural Tourism DC** (202-661-7581, www .culturaltourismdc.org), also offers guided tours focusing on historical and artistic elements of the city. Visit their website for specific trail descriptions and maps.

MAP 5 DUPONT CIRCLE

☾ DUPONT CIRCLE
Stake out a patch of green to watch the people – from musicians to office workers – who congregate around the giant fountain in this lively neighborhood hub.

MAP 5 B5 Ⓐ 30 MASSACHUSETTS AND CONNECTICUT AVES. NW

THOMPSON BOAT CENTER
You can join the lively summer scene on the Potomac by renting a kayak, canoe, or rowboat. Or simply watch the local crew-racing teams practice while sipping your morning coffee.

MAP 5 E1 Ⓐ 59 2900 VIRGINIA AVE. NW
202-333-9543

MAP 7 UPPER NORTHWEST

OLMSTED WOODS AND THE BISHOP'S GARDENS
Olmsted Woods – designed by Central Park architect Frederick Law Olmsted – is a five-acre old-growth forest behind the majestic National Cathedral. The terraced Bishop's Gardens, also on the Cathedral grounds, makes for a great pastoral retreat after touring the Gothic, gargoyle-encrusted structure.

MAP 7 C3 Ⓐ 17 WISCONSIN AND MASSACHUSETTS AVES. NW
AT THE NATIONAL CATHEDRAL
202-537-6200 (CATHEDRAL)

MAP 8 | ADAMS MORGAN/WOODLEY PARK

KALORAMA PARK
A favorite among local nannies, this lively neighborhood park is equipped with two playgrounds for both older and younger children.

MAP 8 D4 ⏺16   KALORAMA RD. AND 19TH ST. NW

⏺ ROCK CREEK NATIONAL PARK
This 1,755-acre swath of forest flanks Rock Creek and offers respite from crowds, traffic, and summer heat. The bike and bridle paths, hiking trails, tennis courts, playgrounds, and golf course make it the perfect place to work off last night's power dinner.

MAP 8 D1 ⏺14   3435 WILLIAMSBURG LN. NW
202-895-6000   WWW.NPS.GOV/ROCR

OVERVIEW MAP

EAST POTOMAC PARK
Mini-golf, a driving range, an 18-hole public course – one of the country's oldest – and a giant sculpture called *The Awakening* make this park a fun and quirky destination. It's also a great place to see the spring cherry blossoms without the typical crowds.

OVERVIEW MAP F4   OHIO DR. SW
202-426-6841

EAST POTOMAC PARK POOL
This 50-meter outdoor pool is the perfect summer cool-off spot. Swim laps or just splash around in the reflection of Washington's monuments for a small fee (free for D.C. residents with ID, $7 for nonresidents).

OVERVIEW MAP F4   1090 OHIO DR. SW
202-727-6523

MERIDIAN HILL PARK
The lower level of this 12-acre neighborhood park (also known as Malcolm X Park), with its terraced waterfalls, broad stairways, and impressive statuary, looks like an Italian movie set. The upper level is a good spot for Frisbee and soccer, and a lively drumming circle erupts Sunday evenings.

OVERVIEW MAP B4   BTWN. 15TH AND 16TH STS. NW,
EUCLID AND W STS. NW
202-462-7275

THEODORE ROOSEVELT ISLAND
Heavily forested trails surrounding a garden and 17-foot statue of Teddy Roosevelt comprise D.C.'s most sprawling monument: a 91-acre natural preserve. Pretty year-round, it's glorious in autumn.

OVERVIEW MAP D2   GEORGE WASHINGTON PKWY.
(ACCESSIBLE ONLY FROM VIRGINIA)

WASHINGTON WALKS

Whether you're fascinated by haunted houses or local secrets, these walking tours are a fun and informative way to see the city. Most take place weekly April–October; call or visit the website for schedules, descriptions, and meeting locations.

VARIOUS LOCATIONS   202-484-1565   WWW.WASHINGTONWALKS.COM

HOTELS

Trendsetter favorite: **HOTEL PALOMAR,** p. 92

Most romantic hotel: **TABARD INN,** p. 94

Funkiest decor: **HOTEL HELIX,** p. 94

Best pool: **OMNI SHOREHAM HOTEL,** p. 96

Best splurge: **HAY-ADAMS HOTEL,** p. 90

Best views: **HOTEL WASHINGTON,** p. 90

Best for pol-watching: **WILLARD INTERCONTINENTAL,** p. 91

PRICE KEY

$	ROOMS UNDER $200
$$	ROOMS $200-300
$$$	ROOMS OVER $300

MAP 1 **WESTERN MALL/FOGGY BOTTOM**

GEORGE WASHINGTON UNIVERSITY INN *QUAINT* $

Popular with longer-term visitors, the inn gets marks for its stately 18th-century decor and location blocks from the Kennedy Center and Georgetown. Guests can enjoy a collegiate atmosphere, and the suite-style accommodations are an excellent value.

 MAP 1 A2 **①**1   824 NEW HAMPSHIRE AVE. NW
202-337-6620   WWW.GWUINN.COM

☾ HAY-ADAMS HOTEL *GRAND* $$$

One of Washington's finest luxury hotels, this monument to indulgence is a favorite of visiting dignitaries. Rumors that the original owner haunts the premises add a hint of mystery to the stately surroundings – especially in winter.

MAP 1 A5 **①**10   800 16TH ST. NW
202-638-6600 OR 800-424-5054   WWW.HAY-ADAMS.COM

☾ HOTEL WASHINGTON *ROMANTIC* $$

Not only does the city's oldest hotel offer excellent, European-style accommodations for its politico-heavy clientele, it boasts the best views in the city. Even if you're not a guest, order a cocktail and sightsee from the romantic rooftop Sky Terrace.

MAP 1 B6 **①**28   515 15TH ST. NW
202-638-5900 OR 800-424-9540
WWW.HOTELWASHINGTON.COM

SOFITEL LAFAYETTE SQUARE *GRAND* $$$

Offering a downtown location and an on-site translator, Sofitel caters primarily to business travelers who want to be in the center

HOTELS

SCANDAL SCENES

Hotel scandals are a Washington tradition – and Watergate is just the tip of the iceberg. If you're a conspiracy theorist with money to burn, check into the **Hay-Adams Hotel (p. 90),** allegedly the site of Iran-Contra meetings. Back in more innocent times, Clover Adams, the wife of Henry Adams and whose house once stood on part of the hotel's site, shocked her high-society friends by overdosing on cyanide in 1885. (Rumor has it that she still haunts the hallways.) Just down the street at **The Jefferson Washington D.C. (p. 95),** Clinton aide Dick Morris was photographed trysting – and sharing state secrets – with a prostitute in 1996. Farther uptown is the **Hilton Washington (p. 96),** where would-be assassin John Hinckley opened fire on President Ronald Reagan and Press Secretary James Brady in 1981.

of it all. There's nothing frilly here, but the posh ground-floor Café 15 is a swank spot to sip and sup.

`MAP 1` **A6 H 15** 806 15TH ST. NW
202-730-8800 WWW.SOFITEL.COM

◖ WILLARD INTERCONTINENTAL *GRAND* *$$$*
Dark, gilded, and steeped in tradition, this most Washington of hotels maintains a loyal clientele with its gracious service. It is also a historical landmark: "The Battle Hymn of the Republic" and the "I Have a Dream" speech were written within these ornate walls.

`MAP 1` **B6 H 30** 1401 PENNSYLVANIA AVE. NW
202-628-9100
WWW.WASHINGTON.INTERCONTINENTAL.COM

MAP 2 SMITHSONIAN/PENN QUARTER

HOTEL MONACO *CHIC* *$$*
With its grand European lobby, plush decor, and ultra-customized guest rooms, this whimsical downtown accommodation charms with its specialized service. Lanky patrons can request "tall rooms," and even your pooch can get pampered with gourmet doggy snacks.

`MAP 2` **B4 H 22** 700 F ST. NW
202-628-7177 OR 877-202-5411 WWW.MONACO-DC.COM

MAP 3 CAPITOL HILL

DOOLITTLE GUEST HOUSE *GRAND* *$*
This ornate Victorian mansion, with fireplaces, a formal dining room, and private baths, has a view of the Capitol from its lavish sitting room. The daily homemade, organic breakfast is a thoughtful touch.

`MAP 3` **D5 H 13** 506 E. CAPITOL ST.
202-546-6622 WWW.DOOLITTLEHOUSE.COM

HOTEL GEORGE *CHIC* *$$*
Sleek, bold, and wildly popular, this hotel is done up with modern lines and pop art, but actually occupies a 1928 edifice. The cigar-and-billiard room and Bistro Bis restaurant add to the lively atmosphere.

`MAP 3` **B2 H 2** 15 E ST. NW
202-347-4200 WWW.HOTELGEORGE.COM

HYATT REGENCY WASHINGTON ON CAPITOL HILL *CHIC* *$$*
This behemoth Hyatt offers the chain's standard amenities, as well as wireless Internet access in renovated rooms. It stands out for the sensational atrium lobby.

`MAP 3` **C2 H 9** 400 NEW JERSEY AVE. NW
202-737-1234 WWW.WASHINGTONREGENCY.HYATT.COM

HOTELS

MAP 4 GEORGETOWN

THE FOUR SEASONS HOTEL *CHIC* $$$

The Four Seasons imbues historic Georgetown with a breath of modernity; amenities include a three-level fitness club, in-room massage options, and some of the most exotic spa treatments in town – such as the Bali Coconilla body polish.

MAP 4 E6 🄷37 2800 PENNSYLVANIA AVE. NW
202-342-0444 WWW.FOURSEASONS.COM

THE GEORGETOWN INN *ROMANTIC* $$

Located in the heart of Georgetown, this inn mixes elegant Federal-era architecture with top-of-the-line customer service.

MAP 4 E4 🄷18 1310 WISCONSIN AVE. NW
202-333-8900

THE LATHAM HOTEL *ROMANTIC* $$

A favorite among celebrities and overseas visitors, the Latham exudes European style. The hotel's acclaimed Michel Richard Citronelle restaurant gives preferential treatment to guests.

MAP 4 E5 🄷35 3000 M ST. NW
202-726-5000 WWW.THELATHAM.COM

MAP 5 DUPONT CIRCLE

HOTELS

THE DUPONT AT THE CIRCLE *ROMANTIC* $$

Built in 1885, this B&B is perfectly situated on a residential street. Nine ornate rooms offer a quiet break in the big city.

MAP 5 A5 🄷10 1604 19TH ST. NW
202-332-5251 WWW.DUPONTATTHECIRCLE.COM

HILTON WASHINGTON EMBASSY ROW *CHIC* $$$

Across from the Indonesian Embassy, the Hilton is festive with colorful fabrics, art, murals, and a daily international buffet.

MAP 5 B4 🄷18 2015 MASSACHUSETTS AVE. NW
202-265-1600 WWW.HILTON.COM

HOTEL MADERA *CHIC* $$

This pet-friendly boutique is all about unique amenities: Make-your-own martini kits come standard in every room, specialty Screening Rooms boast fully stocked DVD libraries, and Nosh Rooms offer grocery service.

MAP 5 C4 🄷33 1310 NEW HAMPSHIRE AVE. NW
202-296-7600 WWW.HOTELMADERA.COM

🄲 HOTEL PALOMAR *CHIC* $$$

Offering artfully funky ambience that is pure Dupont Circle, this Kimpton Hotels property opened in 2006. The prices are steep

RENAISSANCE MAYFLOWER HOTEL   THE RITZ-CARLTON

but worth it, with amenities such as complimentary wine receptions and in-room spa services.

MAP 5 B4 🅗19   2121 P ST. NW
202-448-1800 OR 877-866-3070
WWW.HOTELPALOMAR-DC.COM

THE MANSION ON O STREET   *ROMANTIC* $$$
One of the Capitol's original architects designed this exquisite 1892 mansion. Filled with art and antiques, the Mansion serves as a hushed retreat for discriminating travelers.

MAP 5 B4 🅗27   2020 O ST. NW
202-496-2000   WWW.OMANSION.COM

ONE WASHINGTON CIRCLE   *QUAINT* $$
This stately property is a regular in power players' Palm Pilots. The spacious, comforting digs include suite-sized rooms, and every room comes with a private balcony overlooking the neighborhood.

MAP 5 D3 🅗47   1 WASHINGTON CIR. NW
202-872-1680 OR 800-424-9671
WWW.THECIRCLEHOTEL.COM

RENAISSANCE MAYFLOWER HOTEL   *GRAND* $$$
Situated close to the White House, this address played host to Calvin Coolidge's 1925 inauguration and has a lovely block-long lobby. A 2004 renovation added high-speed Internet capacity to this Marriott-company hotel.

MAP 5 D6 🅗54   1127 CONNECTICUT AVE. NW
202-347-3000   WWW.MARRIOTT.COM

THE RITZ-CARLTON   *ROMANTIC* $$$
This fashionably located property offers such trademark luxuries as featherbeds with Egyptian cotton sheets. Outside the rooms, guests can contemplate in the courtyard's Japanese garden or reenergize in the premiere fitness facility.

MAP 5 D3 🅗46   1150 22ND ST. NW
202-835-0500   WWW.RITZCARLTON.COM

THE RIVER INN   *CHIC* $$
Not on the river, but pretty close, these boutique-style, apartment-size suites come with full kitchens. The modern design and Dish restaurant will appeal to sophisticated travelers.

MAP 5 E2 🅗60   924 25TH ST. NW
202-337-7600   WWW.THERIVERINN.COM

HOTELS

TABARD INN   *ROMANTIC* $

Frequented by journalists, artists, and congressional types, the 1914 Tabard offers 40 rooms with period furnishings and claw-foot tubs. In keeping with the atmosphere, most rooms don't come with televisions or radios, and the four stories are reachable by stairs only.

MAP 5 C6 42   1739 N ST. NW
202-785-1277   WWW.TABARDINN.COM

THE TOPAZ HOTEL   *CHIC* $$

This decidedly 21st-century boutique hotel offers specialty accommodations such as yoga rooms outfitted with mats and blocks, and energy rooms equipped with exercise machines. Guests enjoying more traditional rooms receive daily horoscopes.

MAP 5 C6 43   1733 N ST. NW
202-393-3000   WWW.TOPAZHOTEL.COM

THE WESTIN EMBASSY ROW   *GRAND* $$$

Historic site of the Fairfax Room, the Westin has been pampering politicians and dignitaries since 1928. Today, patrons can enjoy the chain's signature Heavenly touches for bed and bath.

MAP 5 B4 17   2100 MASSACHUSETTS AVE. NW
202-293-2100   WWW.STARWOOD.COM

MAP 6 | 14TH AND U

THE BEACON HOTEL   *CHIC* $

Ideally located between Dupont Circle and Embassy Row, the Beacon Hotel is quickly becoming a favorite for business travelers, thanks to high-tech rooms with flat-screen TVs and Wi-Fi everywhere. Panoramic views of the city make the rooftop deck a favorite summertime hangout.

MAP 6 D2 40   1615 RHODE ISLAND AVE. NW
202-296-2100   WWW.BEACONHOTELWDC.COM

HAMILTON CROWNE PLAZA HOTEL-WASHINGTON D.C.   *CHIC* $

As regal as it was during the 1920s, this restored hotel with a view of Franklin Park offers modern conveniences in a historical building.

MAP 6 F3 55   1001 14TH ST. NW
202-682-0111   WWW.ICHOTELSGROUP.COM

HOTEL HELIX   *CHIC* $$

This Austin Powers meets the Brady Bunch hotel recalls the swinging '60s, with shag carpeting, psychedelic lighting, and funky furniture perfect for its hipster clientele. Room service can bring up yummy comfort food, such as grilled cheese sandwiches.

MAP 6 D3 42   1430 RHODE ISLAND AVE. NW
202-462-9001   WWW.HOTELHELIX.COM

HOTEL ROUGE *CHIC* $$

At once glam and gimmicky, this boutique hotel attracts a young and adventurous crowd. Specialty rooms come outfitted with audiovisual accessories, computer gadgetry, or a stainless steel kitchenette, depending on whether the theme is "Chill," "Chat," or "Chow."

 D2 ⊕ 39 1315 16TH ST. NW
202-232-8000 OR 800-368-5689
WWW.ROUGEHOTEL.COM

THE JEFFERSON WASHINGTON D.C. *ROMANTIC* $$$

This hotel of choice for Democratic strategists is filled with original art and antiques. The restaurant and lounge — all leather and wood paneling — is fit for a president.

 E2 ⊕ 45 1200 16TH ST. NW
202-347-2200
WWW.THEJEFFERSONWASHINGTONDC.COM

THE MADISON HOTEL *CHIC* $$$

This stunning hotel with white-glove service is a revered D.C. favorite. Adding to the dynamic vibe, local and foreign power brokers and policy makers chew the fat in its bar, restaurants, and lobby.

MAP 6 E3 ⊕ 48 1177 15TH ST. NW
202-862-1600   WWW.THEMADISONDC.COM

MORRISON-CLARK INN *GRAND* $$$

These two 19th-century townhouses mix French country and Victorian pieces under a Chinese mansard roof. Enjoy Southern libations on the veranda during warm-weather months; the historical ambience makes up for the proximity to a less-than-desirable neighborhood.

MAP 6 E5 ⊕ 49 1015 L ST. NW
202-898-1200   WWW.MORRISONCLARK.COM

RENAISSANCE WASHINGTON D.C. HOTEL *CHIC* $$$

This contemporary powerhouse bustles with deal-makers and the high-tech crowd. The lobby can't be beat for reading the *Washington Post* over coffee.

MAP 6 F5 ⊕ 61 999 9TH ST. NW
202-898-9000 OR 800-228-9898   WWW.MARRIOTT.COM

THE ST. REGIS *GRAND* $$$

Reopening after renovations in 2007, the palatial 1926 St. Regis will continue to provide opulence fit for royalty (or a clientele who expects to be treated as such), with such standard amenities as terry robes in every room.

MAP 6 F2 ⊕ 51 923 16TH ST. NW
202-638-2626   WWW.STARWOOD.COM

WYNDHAM WASHINGTON D.C. *CHIC* $

The 12-story atrium lobby is the Wyndham's centerpiece; the hotel's stylish guest rooms, eateries, and ballrooms are all arranged around it.

MAP 6 E3 ⊕ 47 1400 M ST. NW
202-429-1700   WWW.WYNDHAM.COM

HOTELS

ADAM'S INN   SWANN HOUSE

MAP 8 | ADAMS MORGAN/WOODLEY PARK

ADAM'S INN   *QUAINT* $
Fun, friendly, and inexpensive, this bed-and-breakfast beckons visitors with a cheery parlor, comfortable furnishings, and inviting front porch.

MAP 8 C5 Ⓗ 4   1746 LANIER PL. NW
202-745-3600   WWW.ADAMSINN.COM

CHURCHILL HOTEL   *GRAND* $$
This elegant 1906 building makes for a refined stay. The hotel borders a residential neighborhood, but a short stroll down Connecticut Avenue rewards guests with the bustle of Dupont Circle.

MAP 8 E4 Ⓗ 28   1914 CONNECTICUT AVE. NW
202-797-2000   WWW.THECHURCHILLHOTEL.COM

HILTON WASHINGTON   *GRAND* $$
The bustling scene of countless society galas – notably, the glamorous White House Correspondents Dinner – this efficient corporate favorite boasts plenty of ballrooms and a lively bar scene.

MAP 8 E4 Ⓗ 27   1919 CONNECTICUT AVE. NW
202-483-3000 OR 800-445-8667   WWW.HILTON.COM

JURYS NORMANDY INN   *QUAINT* $
A charming little find along Embassy Row, the 75-room Jurys Normandy feels more like a friend's home than an inn. Enjoy a cozy fireplace and free Internet access in the lobby.

MAP 8 E4 Ⓗ 26   2118 WYOMING AVE. NW
202-483-1350
WWW.JURYS-WASHINGTONDC-HOTELS.COM

KALORAMA GUEST HOUSE   *QUAINT* $
This group of renovated Victorian townhouses offers a homey B&B escape, complete with a sunny garden and a fireplace-lit parlor.

MAP 8 D4 Ⓗ 15   1854 MINTWOOD PL. NW
202-667-6369   WWW.KALORAMAGUESTHOUSE.COM

◖ OMNI SHOREHAM HOTEL   *GRAND* $$$
Adjacent to Rock Creek Park, the quiet, art deco Omni is not for party animals, despite its proximity to the zoo. Seasoned travelers

HOTELS

will appreciate the gilded lobby, four-poster beds, luxe pool, and sprawling gardens.

MAP 8 **C2** 🕀 **2**   2500 CALVERT ST. NW
202-234-0700   WWW.OMNIHOTELS.COM

SWANN HOUSE   *ROMANTIC*   *$$*
Located on a residential street, this gorgeous Victorian offers B&B individuality, such as themed rooms, without the overly familiar aspects (all rooms have private baths). The courtyard swimming pool is a welcome rejuvenator in the heat of summer.

MAP 8 **F6** 🕀 **41**   1808 NEW HAMPSHIRE AVE. NW
202-265-4414   WWW.SWANNHOUSE.COM

THE WINDSOR INN   *ROMANTIC*   *$*
Formerly an apartment building, this B&B boasts original art deco details in its lobby and 46 rooms that range from spartan economy to well-appointed suites.

MAP 8 **E6** 🕀 **32**   1842 16TH ST. NW
202-667-0300   WWW.WINDSOREMBASSYINNS.COM

OVERVIEW MAP

MANDARIN ORIENTAL   *GRAND*   *$$$*
This posh business-traveler favorite sprung up on Washington's waterfront in 2004. Offering panoramic views, a gourmet restaurant, and on-site spa and fitness facilities, it's an elegant landmark in an overlooked neighborhood.

OVERVIEW MAP **E4**   1330 MARYLAND AVE. SW
202-554-8588   WWW.MANDARIN-ORIENTAL.COM

HOTELS

CITY ESSENTIALS

AIRPORTS

Three major airports serve the Washington metropolitan area: Dulles International (IAD, www.metwashairports .com/Dulles), Reagan National (DCA, www.metwash airports.com/reagan), and Baltimore-Washington International (BWI, www.bwiairport.com). The D.C. Metro system only directly services Reagan National Airport.

The Washington Flyer Coach Service Bus (703-661-6655, www.washfly.com) provides ground transportation between Dulles and the West Falls Church Metro station. Tickets are sold right before you exit the terminal at Dulles and curbside, credit card only, at the Metro station. The cost is $9 one-way or $16 round-trip.

Amtrak (800-872-7245, www.amtrak.com) and the Maryland Area Rail Commuter train (MARC, 800-325-7245, www.mtamaryland.com, weekdays only) travel between Baltimore-Washington International and D.C.'s Union Station. On the lower level, you can catch the free shuttle from the airport to the train station. There's also the Washington Metropolitan Area Transit Authority's Express Metrobus service between the airport and the Greenbelt Metro station. The BWI Express/B30 bus runs every 40 minutes. Bus fare is $3, which is paid on the bus. For more information, call 202-637-7000 or visit www.wmata.com.

If you take a taxi to the airport, expect to pay about $50 for a ride to Dulles, $13 to Reagan National, and $65 to BWI. Additionally, several shuttle services offer transport between the airports and hotel locations in Washington D.C. If taking a shuttle or limousine to the airport, remember to call 24 hours ahead to arrange for a pick-up.

SUPERSHUTTLE 800-258-3826

ARRIVING BY TRAIN

Washington D.C.'s Union Station serves passengers

arriving on Amtrak (800-872-7245, www.amtrak.com) as well as Virginia Railway Express (800-743-3873, www.vre.org) and Maryland's MARC trains (800-325-7245, www.mtamaryland.com). Union Station also connects to the Red Line of the Metro (202-637-7000, www.wmata.com) for destinations within the D.C. area.

UNION STATION
MAP 3 B3 50 MASSACHUSETTS AVE. NE
202-289-1908

ARRIVING BY BUS

Bus transport to and from major East Coast cities is a reliable and cost-effective way to travel. Greyhound (www.greyhound.com) offers tickets to/from New York City (buy tickets at least one week in advance) starting at $23 one-way. The D.C. Greyhound station is located two blocks north of Union Station. A surge of "Chinatown" buses that travel to D.C., New York, Boston, and Philadelphia has made bus travel even more affordable: Apex Bus (888-688-0898, www.apexbus.com) and Washington Deluxe (866-287-6932, www.washny.com) both offer low-fare, reliable transport from various pick-up points in the city.

GREYHOUND BUS TERMINAL
MAP 3 B3 1005 1ST ST. NE
202-289-5154

PUBLIC TRANSPORTATION

Known locally as the Metro, Washington's Metrorail (202-637-7000, www.wmata.com) is a fun ride – clean and quiet, with a space-age feel. There is an information kiosk at every station entrance, and station managers are happy to give directions. However, be prepared for some mighty steep escalators at certain stations; one of the world's longest escalators (230 feet) is at the Forest Glen station on the Red Line.

The Metro runs 5 A.M.-midnight Sunday–Thursday and 7 A.M.-3 A.M. on Friday and Saturday. Be aware that at many stations, the last train departs before closing time. The Metro does not have a stop in Georgetown; however, you can exit at the Rosslyn stop (Orange and Blue Lines) and walk across the Key Bridge, or for an additional $0.35 you can transfer to a Metrobus (be sure to pick up a bus transfer as you enter or exit the Metro).

Fares range $1.35-3.90 depending on the length of the ride. One-day, unlimited ride passes cost $6.50. (Note:

These day passes are only good after 9:30 A.M. on weekdays, but are good all day on Saturday, Sunday, and federal holidays.) A seven-day, truly unlimited pass costs $32.50. Both these passes are good for Metrorail rides only; they do not cover Metrobus fares.

D.C. also recently introduced the Circulator, a new express bus service that links up the National Mall, Southwest Waterfront, Union Station, the convention center, and Georgetown on two easy-to-use bus lines. The fare is $1, and the buses run 7 A.M.–9 P.M. daily (202-962-1423, www.dccirculator.com). There's a third route that covers the Smithsonian/National Gallery of Art loop that runs 9:30 A.M.–6 P.M.

For a map of the Metrorail system, pick up a free Pocket Guide at any station kiosk. Bus route maps are available in CVS pharmacies throughout the city and at the Metro Center sales office at 12th and F Streets NW.

TAXIS

Washington taxis charge by zones – there are eight in the city – rather than by miles. The base fare for one zone is $5; crossing into another zone increases the fare. (There is a $1.50 surcharge per passenger and a $1 surcharge for rush-hour fares.) Read the posted rate card inside the cab to avoid being cheated, something not uncommon in Washington. Hailing a cab is easy downtown, but the farther you get from a busy area, the less likely it is that you will find one. Cabs are plentiful around hotels, Union Station, and the airports. You can also phone ahead to have one meet you, but this service adds a $2 fee to your fare if you call Diamond Cab or Yellow Cab. Red Top does not charge a fee.

DIAMOND CAB 202-387-6200

RED TOP CAB 202-328-3333

YELLOW CAB 202-544-1212

DRIVING AND RENTING A CAR

Though the layout of D.C. is rather straightforward – state-named streets branching from the U.S. Capitol Building like spokes on a wheel, with lettered and numbered streets in a grid pattern – driving in D.C. is a thankless task, and the notorious bumper-to-bumper traffic can reduce even the most hardened native to tears. In addition, some heavily traveled thoroughfares, such as Rock Creek Parkway, become one-way during rush hour, which can be frustrating for people unfamiliar with the area.

In addition, parking is extremely difficult in Washington, especially in popular tourist areas such as the Mall, Georgetown, and Dupont Circle. Too few spaces and too much traffic make finding a place to park frustrating and time consuming. Privately owned parking lots abound. While costly, they may save you money in the long run; parking enforcement is serious business in the capital city, with heavy fines levied for violations. Metro-operated lots require payment using a SmarTrip card (reusable plastic fare cards that you can keep adding money to) during the week, but are free on weekends and federal holidays. Your best bet is to use public transportation.

If you do decide to drive, all of the major car rental chains are represented in Washington. Find them clustered together at the airports, with branches throughout the city. If you are traveling at a busy time of year, be sure to make your reservation well in advance.

ENTERPRISE RENT-A-CAR 800-261-7331 (Dulles), 202-393-0900 (downtown)

HERTZ RENT A CAR 800-654-3131 (Dulles and Reagan), 202-842-0819 (downtown)

THRIFTY CAR RENTAL 877-283-0898 (Dulles), 202-371-0485 (downtown)

VISITOR INFORMATION

The Washington D.C. Convention and Tourism Corporation (202-789-7000, www.washington.org) is the principal tourist organization in the city. Maps, brochures, and other information are available at the visitors center. There are also fleets of hospitality teams positioned throughout downtown, ready to answer questions, offer advice, and distribute free maps. Look for the red baseball caps (202-638-3232, www.downtowndc.org).

WASHINGTON D.C. VISITOR INFORMATION CENTER
MAP 2 B2 RONALD REAGAN BUILDING, 1300 PENNSYLVANIA AVE. NW
202-328-4748

WEATHER

The best time to visit D.C. is during the transitional seasons of fall and spring, when the temperatures remain comfortable – especially March and early April, when the city's cherry blossoms are in full bloom on the Tidal Basin. Otherwise, think warm and humid; even winter brings more than a few days of balmy weather. Summer is long, extending mid-May–late September. July and August are characterized by hot, muggy days with temperatures in the 90s, punctuated by afternoon thunderstorms. Serious cold shows up in January and February, although rarely do temperatures dip below freezing. The city is unprepared for such inclement weather; even a light dusting of snow snarls traffic. A major snowstorm every few years delights area children but closes down everything. For the current temperature and local forecast, call 202-936-1212.

HOURS

Despite its cosmopolitan veneer, Washington is a sleepy Southern town during the week, with most restaurants, coffeehouses, and clubs closing long before midnight, though technically last call is at 1:30 A.M. On weekends, the more daring among them remain open until 2:30 A.M. The Metro runs 5 A.M.–midnight Sunday–Thursday, and 7 A.M.–3 A.M. on Friday and Saturday. Additionally, the city slows down in August and during holiday weekends when Congress is out of session. Government buildings are closed on federal holidays, and most monuments are closed on December 25.

FESTIVALS AND EVENTS

JANUARY/FEBRUARY

Martin Luther King Day: Speakers recite the legendary "I Have a Dream" speech at the Lincoln Memorial. Third Monday in January. (Lincoln Memorial, 202-426-6841)

MARCH

Cherry Blossom Festival: Tourists and residents alike celebrate the 1912 gift of 3,000 cherry trees from Tokyo to the citizenry of D.C. Two unpredictable weeks in late March or early April. (Tidal Basin, 202-661-7584, www.nationalcherryblossomfestival.org)

Smithsonian Kite Festival: This airborne celebration showcases kite-flying masters and a traditional

Japanese *rokkaku* kite battle. First day of the Cherry Blossom Festival. (National Mall, 202-357-3030, www .kitefestival.org)

APRIL

White House Easter Egg Roll: Children roll eggs across the White House Lawn and meet the President. Call ahead for ticket information. (White House Lawn, 1600 Pennsylvania Ave. NW, 202-456-7041, www.whitehouse .gov/easter)

Filmfest DC: Once a year, D.C. channels the spirit of Cannes. This film festival showcases hundreds of new documentaries, feature films, and shorts from around the world. Late April and early May. (Multiple screening locations, 202-628-FILM, www.filmfestdc.org)

MAY

Shakespeare Free for All: The Shakespeare Theatre Company hosts a series of free performances of one of the bard's plays at Carter Barron Amphitheatre in Rock Creek National Park. Day-of-performance tickets are available at the box office and in two downtown locations; advanced tickets are also available. Late May–early June. (16th St. and Colorado Ave. NW, 202-547-1122, www.shakespearetheatre.org)

JUNE

Capital Pride: D.C.'s nine-day pride festival includes a jubilant parade and raucous street festival. Mid-June. (Various locations, 202-797-3514, www.capitalpride.org)

Smithsonian Folklife Festival: This annual celebration brings the storytellers, cuisine, artists, and musicians of different countries, cultures, and regions to the National Mall. Past festivals have showcased everything from music in Latino culture to maritime communities of the mid-Atlantic. Late June and early July. (National Mall, 202-275-1150, www.folklife.si.edu)

JULY

Independence Day Celebration: D.C. lights up for the Fourth of July. A free-to-the-public concert special features the National Symphony Orchestra and is followed by a spectacular fireworks display over the Washington Monument. July 4. (U.S. Capitol/National Mall)

SEPTEMBER

D.C. Blues Society Annual Festival: The D.C. Blues Society hosts this annual kickin' blues extravaganza at the Carter Barron Amphitheatre. Admission is free.

Early September. (Carter Barron Amphitheatre in Rock Creek Park, 202-962-0112, www.dcblues.org)

The Adams Morgan Day Festival: The main strip in this hip neighborhood is closed off to motorized traffic. Food stalls are set up, stages host local bands, and vendors hawk their trinkets. Saturdays are reserved for sporting events and kid-oriented activities, while Sundays turn into a raucous street party. Second weekend of September. (18th St. and Columbia Ave. NW, www.adamsmorgandayfestival.org)

OCTOBER

Marine Corps Marathon: Whether you're a participant or a sidewalk supporter, this "People's Marathon" has prompted a weekend-long celebration since 1976. Late October. (Starts on Rt. 110 near Arlington Memorial Bridge in Arlington, VA, 800-786-8762, www.marinemarathon.com)

NOVEMBER

Veterans Day at Arlington National Cemetery: Attend the annual wreath-laying ceremony – a moving tribute to our nation's veterans. November 11. (Arlington National Cemetery, 703-607-8000, www.arlingtoncemetery.org)

DECEMBER

National Christmas Tree Lighting: Thousands of spectators have flocked to the Ellipse, south of the White House grounds, to witness the lighting of the National Christmas Tree. Early December. (Ellipse, 202-208-1631, www.nps.gov/whho/pageant)

DISABLED ACCESS

All Smithsonian museums have at least one wheelchair-accessible entrance, most of them on the Mall side. Wheelchairs are available for use in most museums on a first-come, first-served basis. Most restaurants, bars, theaters, and all federal buildings are equipped with restrooms accessible for travelers with disabilities. Street corners throughout the city have graded curbs for wheelchair ease.

Metro buses and subways accommodate travelers with disabilities with elevators, Braille signage, flashing signal lights, and enhanced announcements. More than 70 percent of the bus fleet is equipped with lifts, which means an automated platform lowers to the curb to facilitate boarding for passengers in wheelchairs. To be sure one of these buses comes to your stop, call 202-962-1825 before 3 P.M. on the preceding afternoon.

SAFETY

Follow the rules for any bustling major city: Always lock your car, hold tight to your belongings, and keep your wits about you. Avoid dark alleys, and don't dawdle in deserted downtown areas at night. Be more attentive to your surroundings in Adams Morgan and Capitol Hill; common crimes are street robbery and car theft.

HEALTH AND EMERGENCY SERVICES

As in most cities in the United States, dialing 911 will connect you with police and fire emergency teams immediately. The following hospitals have 24-hour emergency rooms:

GEORGETOWN UNIVERSITY HOSPITAL
MAP 4 B1   3800 RESERVOIR RD. NW
202-444-2000

GEORGE WASHINGTON UNIVERSITY HOSPITAL
MAP 1 A2   901 23RD ST. NW
202-715-4000

PHARMACIES

CVS is the principal chain of pharmacies in D.C., with many branches throughout the city.

CVS PHARMACIES
MAP 1 A4   1990 K ST. NW
202-223-8735
MAP 6 E4   1199 VERMONT AVE. NW
202-628-0720
MAP 8 C6   1700 COLUMBIA RD. NW
202-234-8601

MEDIA AND COMMUNICATIONS

In this era of cell phones, pay phones can still be found on many street corners, but more than a few are apt to be out of service, broken, or otherwise unusable. More reliable are those inside museums, Metro stations, and hotel lobbies. A local call is $0.50; an emergency call to 911 is free.

Etiquette requires you to turn off all electronic devices in theaters and most restaurants and music clubs.

For post office locations and hours of operation, call 800-275-8777. A centrally located post office, not far from the White House, is the Ben Franklin station.

BENJAMIN FRANKLIN STATION
MAP 2 C2   12TH ST. AND PENNSYLVANIA AVE. NW

Two daily papers, natural rivals at opposite ends of the political spectrum, keep the locals informed: the

Washington Post and the *Washington Times.* The *City Paper,* which details entertainment and nightlife, and the *Washington Blade,* which serves the gay and lesbian community, are free weeklies available at area bookstores and coffee houses.

If you don't have access to the Internet at your hotel, you can access the Internet at certain locations of Kinko's, a full-service print/copy shop serving the student and business community. Internet cafés are few and far between, as they are not part of the city's culture.

KINKO'S

 MAP 4 E3 3329 M ST. NW
202-965-1414

MAP 6 F2 1612 K ST. NW
202-466-3777

CYBERSTOPCAFÉ

MAP 6 C2 1513 17TH ST. NW
202-234-2470

SMOKING

As of January 2007, smoking is banned in restaurants, bars, and other public places, though some establishments categorized as smoke shops, or those who have filed the necessary petitions and paperwork, may be exempt. Exemptions include outdoor areas, hotel rooms, retail tobacco outlets, and cigar bars. Smoking is also prohibited in the Smithsonian museums and government buildings.

TIPPING

A general rule is to tip 15–20 percent of the final bill in restaurants and taxis. At the airport, or in a hotel, the porter or baggage handler usually receives $2 per bag.

DRY CLEANERS

CATHEDRAL CUSTOM CLEANERS

MAP 8 A2 3000 CONNECTICUT AVE. NW
202-234-1288

GEORGETOWN CLEANERS

MAP 4 E5 1070 31ST ST. NW
202-965-9655

LOGAN CLEANERS

MAP 6 D3 1408 14TH ST. NW
202-462-2502

LUSTRE CLEANERS OF CAPITOL HILL

MAP 3 E4 311 PENNSYLVANIA AVE. SE
202-547-1311

STREET INDEX

TRANSIT INDEX

INDEX

RESTAURANTS INDEX

HOTELS INDEX

CONTRIBUTORS TO THE THIRD EDITION

KARA BASKIN *Introduction, A Day in Washington D.C., Neighborhoods, Restaurants, Shops, Hotels*
Kara Baskin is an assistant editor at *The New Republic* magazine in Washington D.C., where she writes about pop culture. She is also a literary editor at the Gail Ross Literary Agency and a managing editor of the Jewish Rock and Roll Hall of Fame. She has written about food, travel, and culture in the Washington area for a variety of national and mid-Atlantic publications.

NATHAN BORCHELT *Nightlife, Recreation, City Essentials*
Nathan Borchelt is a freelance writer living in Washington D.C.

KATHLEEN RELLIHAN *Sights, Museums and Galleries, Performing Arts*
Kathleen Rellihan is a writer and editor living in the revitalized Columbia Heights neighborhood of Washington D.C. She is a network editor for AOL and has contributed to a variety of lifestyle and entertainment magazines in the metro area such as *Northern Virginia, On Tap,* and *Baltimore.*

CONTRIBUTORS TO PREVIOUS EDITIONS
Kara Baskin, Scott Deckman, Sybil Dunlop, Karen Fox, Alexandra Greeley, Matt McMillen, Jonathan Miller, Andrea Rouda

PHOTO CREDITS

MOON METRO WASHINGTON D.C.
THIRD EDITION

Avalon Travel Publishing
An Imprint of Avalon Publishing Group, Inc.

Text and maps © 2007 by Avalon Travel Publishing
All rights reserved.

Transit Map: © 2006 Washington Metropolitan Area Transit Authority

Some photos and illustrations are used by permission and are the
property of the original copyright owners.

ISBN-10: 1-56691-978-9
ISBN-13: 978-1-56691-978-4
ISSN: 1539-090X

Editors: Grace Fujimoto, Shari Husain
Series Manager: Erin Raber
Interior Design: Jacob Goolkasian
Map Design: Mike Morgenfeld
Production Coordinator: Darren Alessi
Graphics Coordinator: Stefano Boni
Cartographer: Suzanne Service
Map Editor: Albert Angulo
Proofreader: Amy Scott
Street Indexer: Andrew Lowder

Front cover photo: Lincoln Memorial, Washington, USA
  © Richard Nowitz / Getty Images

Printed in China through Imago Services, Ltd., Hong Kong

Printing History
1st edition – 2002
3rd edition – April 2007
5 4 3 2 1

Please send all feedback about this book to:
Moon Metro Washington D.C.
Avalon Travel Publishing
1400 65th Street, Suite 250
Emeryville, CA 94608, USA
email: feedback@moon.com
website: www.moon.com

www.moon.com

MOON HANDBOOKS

MOON METRO

MOON OUTDOORS

**TAKE A HIKE
LOS ANGELES**
Hikes within Two Hours of the City

ANN MARIE BROWN & JULIE SHEER

**OREGON
FISHING**

CRAIG SCHUHMANN

**WASHINGTON
CAMPING**
The Complete Guide to Tent and RV Camping

TOM STIENSTRA

MOON LIVING ABROAD

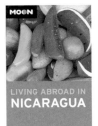

**LIVING ABROAD IN
NICARAGUA**

RANDALL WOOD & JOSHUA BERMAN

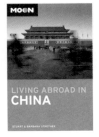

**LIVING ABROAD IN
CHINA**

STUART & BARBARA STROTHER

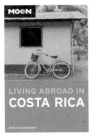

**LIVING ABROAD IN
COSTA RICA**

ERIN VAN RHEENEN

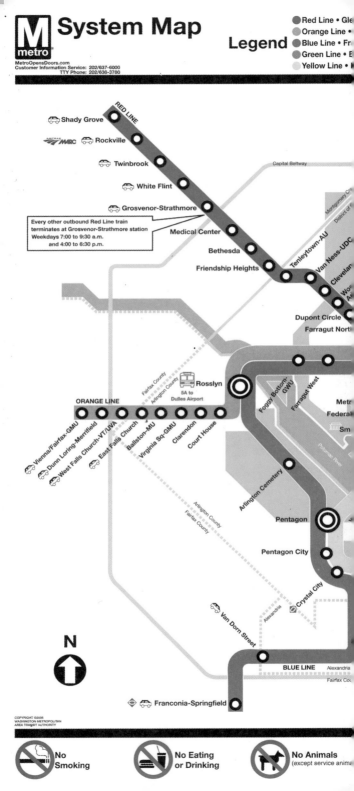